ISSUES THAT CONCERN YOU

Money Management

Jill Hamilton, *Book Editor*

GREENHAVEN PRESS

A part of Gale, Cengage Learning

GALE
CENGAGE Learning™

Detroit • New York • San Francisco • New Haven, Conn • Waterville, Maine • London

Christine Nasso, *Publisher*
Elizabeth Des Chenes, *Managing Editor*

For more information, contact:
Greenhaven Press
27500 Drake Rd.
Farmington Hills, MI 48331-3535
Or you can visit our Internet site at gale.cengage.com

LIBRARY OF CONGRESS CATALOGING-IN-PUBLICATION DATA

Money management / Jill Hamilton, editor.
    p. cm. -- (Issues that concern you)
  Includes bibliographical references and index.
  ISBN 978-0-7377-4496-5 (hardcover)
  1. Teenagers--Finance, Personal. I. Hamilton, Jill.
  HG179.M5934 2009
  332.0240083'5--dc22

            2009009479

Printed in the United States of America
1 2 3 4 5 6 7 13 12 11 10 09

CONTENTS

A 2008 article in *The New York Times* was headlined: "Are We a Nation of Financial Illiterates?" Unfortunately, in many ways, the answer is proving to be yes. Poll after poll comes up with grim statistics about Americans' lack of financial knowledge. In a 2008 survey by TNS Global, a market research company, only 35 percent of respondents could correctly estimate how interest compounds over time and more than half did not understand how minimum payments are calculated and applied to a principal balance. "If we fail to act now to improve economic literacy in this country, our children will be at risk for crippling personal debt, costly decisions at work and at home, and lack competitive skills in a fast-paced global economy," reported the National Council on Economic Education (NCEE) in 2009.

The consequences of widespread financial illiteracy hit home for many Americans in 2008 and 2009. The mortgage meltdown, for example, was fueled in part by home buyers who did not understand how a variable interest rate loan could raise their payments to unmanageable levels if interest rates rose. When mortgage rates rose, many people could not make their payments and were forced to default on their home loans. In general, a lack of understanding about credit card debt and the problems of just making minimum payments has led to a situation in which one in four Americans report having "unmanageable levels of debt." The personal savings rate for Americans during the last few years has been zero or even negative. According to *The Christian Science Monitor*, only 42 percent of adults in the United States have calculated how much money they will need for retirement. Only half of full-time workers participate in their employer's retirement-saving plan.

The lowest financial literacy is found in people with low education levels, women, and certain minority groups; this lack of financial knowledge can have disastrous effects on their lives. Financial systems are often set up in ways that harm the people who do not

According to numerous polls, many young people leave high school financially illiterate.

understand the rules, and are least able to pay. People who do not understand the basics of balancing a checking account, for example, may overdraw their account, and be subject to higher fees. Many banks also charge higher fees when customers' accounts dip below a minimum balance. And people who get behind on any kind of payment, such as medical bills, credit card loans, or car loans, get charged penalty fees and higher interest rates. People who are poor often do not have bank accounts and make use of financial products that cost more, such as money orders, payday loan services, and check cashing businesses.

Young people are another group affected by financial illiteracy. A survey by the Jump$tart Coalition for Personal Financial Literacy found that the average high school senior could only answer about half the questions on a basic financial knowledge test. Many young people leave high school without a savings plan, unable to balance a checkbook, or decipher the various credit card offers they receive. Many find themselves starting out their adult lives already in debt. In fact, people under twenty-five are the fastest growing group filing for bankruptcy.

Most financial experts agree that Americans need far more financial education. At press time, only three states mandated a full semester of personal finance education in high school. Seventeen states offer lessons in personal finance, but only as a part of other subjects such as math or social studies. The rest offer nothing at all. Many advocates say that schools in every state need to offer dedicated personal finance classes to all students.

Government is taking other steps to improve literacy. As the economy tumbled in 2008, President George W. Bush started the President's Council on Financial Literacy. The group's first actions were to work out a financial literacy curriculum for middle school students and to support a Financial Literacy Corps, which would match financial expert volunteers with people having financial difficulties. New York City mayor Michael Bloomberg created an Office of Financial Empowerment. The office has helped people start bank accounts and found philanthropists to match their first contributions to the accounts. The office also worked hard to ensure that New Yorkers were aware that firms offering "rapid refunds" on tax returns were, in fact, actually offering loans. Since 2004, Congress has considered—but as of press time had not passed—a "KIDS Account" bill which would give each child a five-hundred-dollar savings account at birth.

Whether increased government and school programs have a positive impact on financial literacy remains to be seen. Combating financial illiteracy is just one of the issues related to money management that students face today. Authors in this anthology also examine money management issues such as credit cards, allowances, and teen jobs. In addition, the volume contains appendixes to help the reader understand and explore the topic, including a thorough bibliography and a list of organizations to contact for further information. The appendix titled "What You Should Know About Money Management" offers facts about young people and their spending, saving, and working habits. The appendix "What You Should Do About Money Management" offers tips for readers looking to educate themselves and others on money issues. With all these features, *Issues That Concern You: Money Management* provides an excellent resource for everyone interested in this issue.

ONE

Money Management: The Basics

FDIC Consumer News

The following viewpoint provides an overview on money management for teens. It covers the basics of how to save money, choose a checking or savings account, and points out the benefits of interest payments, or what the financial world calls "the miracle of compounding." For more advanced savers, there are also tips on how to invest in stocks, bonds, and mutual funds, and advice on becoming a savvy shopper. The selection was excerpted from a Federal Deposit Insurance Corporation (FDIC) publication on money management for teens. The FDIC is an independent agency of the federal government formed in 1933 after bank failures of the 1920s and 1930s shook confidence in the banking industry. The FDIC promotes public confidence by insuring deposits in banks and limiting the effect of bank failures on the larger economy.

Everyone can use a little guidance on how to save more money. Here are some suggestions for simple things you can do.

Set goals. "Saving money now for use in the future gets easier if you know what you want and how much you'll need," said Janet Kincaid, FDIC Senior Consumer Affairs Officer. It helps to set savings goals you can easily achieve. If you want to buy a

"Start Smart: Money Management for Teens," *FDIC Consumer News*, Summer 2006. Reproduced by permission.

$500 item within the next year, plan to save $50 a month for 10 months, which is just $12.50 a week. (We're not including any "interest" you could earn on your savings.)

Have a strategy for saving money. Every time you receive money—from your allowance, a gift, a summer job or some other source—try to automatically put some of it into savings instead of spending it. That approach to saving money is known as "paying yourself first."

Here's one suggestion: Consider putting about 25 percent ($1 out of every $4) or more into savings that you intend to let build for a few years, perhaps for a down payment on your first car. Separately you can save a similar amount of money for clothes, video games, electronics or other items you might want to buy within the next few months. With what's left, keep some handy for spending money (maybe for snacks or a movie) and also consider donating some of your money to charity.

Cut back, not out. Are you spending $5 a week on snacks? If you save $2 by cutting back, after a year you'll have $104 to put in a savings or investment account that earns interest.

A Small Savings Account Can Get Big over Time

People who put even a small amount of money into a savings account as often as they can and leave it untouched for years may be amazed at how big the account grows. The reason? A combination of saving as much as possible on a regular basis and the impact of interest payments (what the financial world calls "the miracle of compounding").

Here's how you can slowly build a large savings account and experience the miracle of compounding.

Let's say you put money into a savings account that pays you interest every month. After the first month, the interest payment will be calculated based on the money you put in. But the next time the bank pays you interest, it will calculate the amount based on your original deposit plus the interest you received the previous month. Later, that larger, combined amount will earn more interest, and after many years it becomes a much larger sum of money. The earnings are called compound interest.

How $50 Can Grow

You can earn even more in compound interest if you make deposits regularly and stretch to put in as much as you can and leave it untouched. . . . [For example, let's look at] a savings account [that] started with $50 and earned interest at a rate of 3.5 percent each month. If you add just $10 each month, the account can grow nicely to $714 after five years.

If you instead put in a slightly higher amount—$15 each month—you'd have a balance of $1,042 after five years. But if you had increased your deposits to $50 a month, those extra dollars plus the compounding of interest would give you a balance of $3,333 after five years.

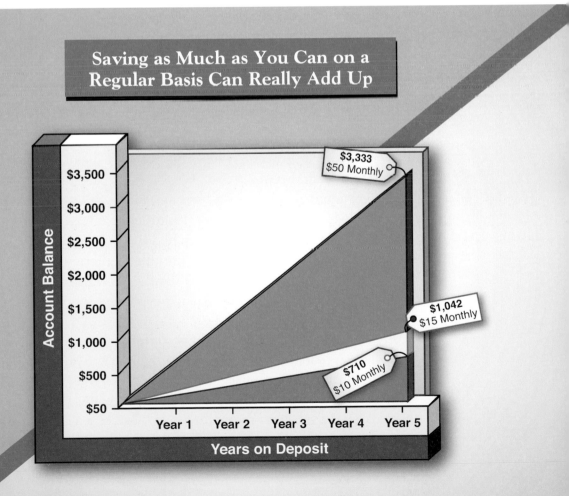

Saving as Much as You Can on a Regular Basis Can Really Add Up

$3,333
$50 Monthly

$1,042
$15 Monthly

$710
$10 Monthly

Account Balance: $3,500 · $3,000 · $2,500 · $2,000 · $1,500 · $1,000 · $500 · $50

Year 1 · Year 2 · Year 3 · Year 4 · Year 5

Years on Deposit

Taken from: "Start Smart: Money Management for Teens," *FDIC Consumer News*, Summer 2006.

How to Choose and Use a Checking or Savings Account

You probably started saving money years ago in a piggy bank and may now have another favorite place at home to stash your cash. That's fine for smaller bills and coins, but what if you've got checks and large sums of money from birthday gifts or your job? Maybe your parents (or other trusted adults) have been keeping your money in their bank accounts. Now may be a good time to talk with them about opening your own bank account which, if you are under 18, you'll probably have to do with their help.

There are lots of good reasons for opening a checking or savings account at a bank, including these:

Safety. Money in the bank is better protected against loss or theft than it is at home. And if the bank has financial troubles and goes out of business, your FDIC-insured money will be fully protected.

Different Ways to Save

Banks offer several different ways to save money and earn interest, which is what banks pay customers to keep their money in the bank. "It's also less tempting to spend your money if it's in the bank rather than in your room," said Sachie Tanaka, an FDIC Consumer Affairs Specialist.

One example of a common bank product is a "certificate of deposit," which enables you to earn a higher interest rate the longer you leave the money untouched in the bank, but these accounts usually require a large amount of money (perhaps $1,000 or more) to open. But many banks also offer special savings accounts designed just for young people and can be opened with very little money.

Easy access. Bank customers have different ways to send or receive their money—from going to the bank to writing checks or using the Internet from home. Some banks even have "branches" at schools. If your parents approve, you also may want to start using a debit card to make purchases. It looks like a credit card but you won't pay interest or get into debt because the money is automatically deducted from your bank account.

Many banks offer their teen customers easy access to banking, as well as special savings accounts designed for them.

Be a Savvy Saver

Whether you open a checking or savings account, it pays to be smart in how you choose and use the account. Here are some suggestions:

Shop around for a good deal before you open an account. Banks usually offer several accounts to choose from with different features, fees, interest rates, opening balance requirements and so on. These accounts also may differ significantly from bank to bank. Some banks have special accounts for teens and even younger kids featuring parental controls on withdrawals.

It's usually best to choose an account that takes very little money to start and involves low fees or no fees for having the account. "The fees charged may be more important than any interest you may earn on the account, especially if the account has a small balance," said James Williams, an FDIC Consumer Affairs Specialist.

Keep your account records up to date. Record *all* transactions— deposits and withdrawals.

Pay attention to your bank statements and immediately report any errors. If your account has a minimum balance requirement, avoid going below it. Your bank may charge you a fee, which would mean less money in your account.

Use the account responsibly. Even a "free" checking account can involve some fees, such as when you use another bank's ATM to withdraw money, so do your best to keep costs down. Also, never share your account numbers, bank cards or passwords with friends or strangers—this could give them access to your money.

The Ins and Outs of Investing

Investments can be attractive alternatives to bank savings accounts as a way to earn money. They come in different varieties, and they may be sold by banks as well as by brokerage firms and other financial institutions. You can make money on investments—often more than you can earn on bank deposit accounts—by selling them for more than you paid for them or by earning dividends or interest.

But investments also involve more risks than bank deposits, including the possibility that you could lose some or all of your money if the investment doesn't perform well.

Some of the more popular types of investments to consider (with a parent or guardian if you are under 18) include:

- *Stocks*, which are shares in the ownership of a company. If the company does well, you might be able to sell your stock for more than you paid for it. But if the company does poorly and you want to sell your stock, you might lose money.

- *Bonds*, which represent a promise by a company or another organization to pay a specific interest rate for money you leave with it for a certain time period.
- *Mutual funds*, which are professionally-managed collections of money from many different investors. Each mutual fund buys a variety of stocks, bonds or other investments. Some mutual fund accounts can be opened for an initial investment of $250 or less.

Know the Risks

You might find it interesting to invest in companies whose products or services you use and like. But it's especially important to remember that investments involve risks and are not insured by the FDIC—not even the investments sold at FDIC-insured banks.

"When you're willing to take some risks for your money to grow—and you believe it won't hurt you if some or all of your money is lost—then you're ready to move from saving to investing," said James Williams, an FDIC Consumer Affairs Specialist. "But before any young person wants to invest money it's important for them to consult with their parents, do some research and consider getting professional advice."

Ways to Cut Spending

Do you want to find ways to stretch your money, so it goes farther and is there when you really need it? Here are some suggestions for knowing how much money you have, how much you need for expenditures, and how to reach your goals by cutting back on what you spend.

1. Practice self-control. To avoid making a quick decision to buy something just because you saw it featured on display or on sale:

- Make a shopping list before you leave home and stick to it.
- *Before* you go shopping, set a spending limit (say, $5 or $10) for "impulse buys"—items you didn't plan to buy but that got your attention anyway. If you are tempted to spend more than your limit, wait a few hours or a few days and think it over.

- Limit the amount of cash you take with you. The less cash you carry, the less you can spend and the less you lose if you misplace your wallet.

Be a Smart Shopper

2. Research before you buy. To be sure you are getting a good value, especially with a big purchase, look into the quality and the reputation of the product or service you're considering. Read "reviews" in magazines or respected Web sites. Talk to knowledgeable people you trust. Check other stores or go online and compare prices. Look at similar items. This is known as "comparison shopping," and it can lead to tremendous savings and better quality purchases. And if you're sure you know what you want, take advantage of store coupons and mail-in "rebates."

3. Keep track of your spending. This helps you set and stick to limits, what many people refer to as budgeting. "Maintaining a budget may sound scary or complicated, but it can be as simple as having a notebook and writing down what you buy each month," said Janet Kincaid, FDIC Senior Consumer Affairs Officer. "Any system that helps you know how much you are spending each month is a good thing."

Small Amounts Add Up

Also pay attention to small amounts of money you spend. "A snack here and a magazine there can quickly add up," said Paul Horwitz, an FDIC Community Affairs Specialist. He suggested that, for a few weeks, you write down every purchase in a small notebook. "You'll probably be amazed at how much you spend without even thinking."

4. Think "used" instead of "new." Borrow things (from the library or friends) that you don't have to own. Pick up used games, DVDs and music at "second-hand" stores around town.

5. Take good care of what you buy. It's expensive to replace things. Think about it: Do you really want to buy the same thing twice?

TWO

Teens Are More Savvy About Money Management than Adults Think

Tina Wells

In the following viewpoint author Tina Wells argues that teens are better at reacting to bad economic times than their parents think, and, in many cases, are better than the adults at adjusting. Wells cites a report that found that teens are spending less than before and, when they do spend, find better deals and are savvy shoppers. She notes that they are also quick to find entrepreneurial ways to earn money, marketing themselves online and finding and filling job niches. Wells is the founder of Buzz Marketing Group, which researches and reports on teen trends.

Here's something that will make financially stressed parents of teenagers across the nation shriek with joy: yes, your teens actually DO care that there is a recession going on. And they are finding ways to curb their spending that could teach a few of us more extravagant adults a thing or two about budgeting with style. They're turning to thrift shops, finding bargains in Target and Forever 21, and, if there's a luxury item they just can't live without, they're trolling the Internet for the best possible deals, and waiting for the price to drop until it falls within a budget they've set for themselves.

Retailers who are marketing to teens and counting on their spending habits being recession proof had better think twice. What was true in the last recession, after the IT bubble burst, is not true today. According to recent research by retail analyst Piper Jaffray, total teen spending on fashion is down 20% compared with [2007]. When they do spend, it's on less expensive brands, like American Eagle and Hollister. This is in stark contrast to a similar survey in 2002, also by Piper Jaffray, which found that teen spending overall was up 23% compared to the previous year, with kids going for higher end name brands like Tommy Hilfiger.

This isn't necessarily true for 'tweens, who tend to rule mom and dad's credit card. But kids in their later teen years, who are responsible for finding their own part-time and summer jobs, are

Teen spending on fashion was down by 20 percent in 2008, compared to 2007, and more teens are becoming savvy bargain hunters.

getting more and more frugal as they head into college. According to that same Piper Jaffray report, they don't have a lot of choice. Their parents are also spending less on their older kids, cutting back on fashion spending by more than 40%, to $883 compared with $1,487 a year.

You could argue that this has something to do with the severity of this recession. It's not abstract. This time around, people are losing their homes. Parents are struggling to pay for their kids' college tuition, but with what? Tuition fees have gone through the roof, the credit crunch is making it next to impossible to obtain student loans at reasonable interest rates, and today's savvy teens are well aware of this.

Teens Are Paying Attention to the Economy

Now more than ever, young people are so plugged in to what's happening around them, they can't help but care. If they do a search for music on AOL, the first thing they see is the news on the site's home page, and they are actually pausing to read the economic headlines. If their parents still have their jobs and aren't going into foreclosure, teens have at least one friend in school whose family is affected by the economic turmoil.

My buzzSpotters [a group of teen trendsetters who report on what is popular with teens] talk about the student loan situation all the time. They've also been bumping up against a brutal job market this summer [2008]. Knowing that college loan money isn't guaranteed anymore, they're looking for part-time work after school and after their summer day jobs. Many are even having trouble finding work, as 20-somethings and college grads grab the jobs at Gap and Starbucks.

It's got to be rough. But here's the good news: Instead of giving up, hanging around the house and playing victim, today's youth are going online and finding ways to network and start their own businesses. I know one buzzSpotter who started a home improvement business with his friend that undercuts the competition by miles. For $500, he painted a customer's brand new condo. And his company name is totally fitting: Affordable Improvements. In fact, I was so impressed I just hired him to do some landscaping

Teen Spending Habits

Spending by Category–All Students	Fall 2007	Spring 2007	Fall 2006	Spring 2006
Video games/systems	5 percent	6 percent	5 percent	4 percent
Music/movies (DVD/CD)	8 percent	9 percent	10 percent	9 percent
Electronics/gadgets	6 percent	6 percent	6 percent	5 percent
Clothing	23 percent	24 percent	23 percent	25 percent
Accessories/personal care/cosmetics	11 percent	13 percent	11 percent	11 percent
Shoes	8 percent	7 percent	7 percent	7 percent
Food	15 percent	15 percent	15 percent	16 percent
Concerts/movies/ sporting events	7 percent	5 percent	6 percent	5 percent
Car	10 percent	8 percent	10 percent	10 percent
Books/magazines	2 percent	2 percent	2 percent	2 percent
Furniture/room accessories	1 percent	1 percent	1 percent	1 percent
Other	3 percent	3 percent	3 percent	4 percent
Total Fashion (clothing, access and footwear)	**42 percent**	**44 percent**	**41 percent**	**43 percent**

Taken from: "Taking Stock with Teens," Piper Jaffray, October 2007. www.piperjaffray.com/2col_largeright.aspx?id=716.

for a fraction of what professional landscapers charge, and he did an amazing job.

I know of other teens who are branching out and offering their services as personal assistants to wealthy families in the neighborhood. They're handling the babysitting, grocery shopping and whatever other errands need to be done. They're finding needs in the marketplace and filling them, and they're marketing themselves through Facebook and Craigslist. Because they've worked so hard for their cash and gone into business for themselves, these "teenpreneurs" are dealing with the idea of budgets for the first time in their lives, and they're being smart about it.

Young People Are Quicker than Adults to React to New Economic Conditions

I have to confess, these young people are adapting to the new economic realities a lot faster than my generation. I'm not letting the cost of gas affect how much I drive, even though I probably should. Sure, I may not spend thousands on the latest Prada bag. I try to curb my spending habits as much as the next person, but the concessions that me and my friends make are small.

No doubt there are still spoiled teens burning through their parents' credit cards, but overall these kids seem to care about so much more than the designer clothes on their backs. They're interested in politics, ending the war in Iraq and doing as much as they can to reduce their carbon footprints and end global warming. They're embarrassed by conspicuous consumption and flashy labels. They're so fabulous and hip that they're setting their own economizing trends, mixing a two-dollar tee shirt with store bought threads and creating unique looks.

Admittedly, none of this thrifty chic among teens is earth shattering news. But in a small way it gives me hope that maybe, just maybe, this generation will do a better job of managing their costs under the weight of the multi-billion dollar deficit that Washington has dumped in their laps. Maybe they're the ones who will be able to fix this mess.

THREE

Overindulged Teens Are Not Savvy About Money Management

Robert J. Samuelson

In the following selection Robert J. Samuelson argues that today's society creates a class of overindulged teens who lack good money sense. He notes several factors that contribute to this. Unlike teens of earlier generations who had to start working as early as age eleven, today's teens have become mostly consumers instead of workers. Such teens have more money than ever to spend but generally have not had to put in the effort of earning it. Teens are also bombarded with a host of media images showing wealth and conspicuous consumption. Such images create an unrealistic lifestyle standard. Parents who provide their children with plenty of material comfort are also part of the problem, notes Samuelson. "The trouble is that today's middle-class children are educated into a doctrine of effortless wealth," he writes. "We parents may make it worse. The very comfort that we try to create for our children may give them the misleading impression that achieving the same for themselves will be more automatic than it is." Samuelson is a contributing editor for *Newsweek* and *The Washington Post*.

One of my bad habits is contemplating my failures as a parent. The evidence of this surrounds me. My teenagers watch too much television and spend too much time on videogames (even though we remove the controllers during the week). Their rooms do not reflect my constant commands that they clean up. Even my wife's stern common sense cannot compensate for all my parental shortcomings. But to my list of defeats now can be added another: money management.

I have failed to instruct my children properly. I know this because I have just finished David Owen's delightful book, "The First National Bank of Dad: The Best Way to Teach Kids About Money." Children should usually receive generous allowances and have more control over their money, says Owen. "If the money

Avid teenage consumers are susceptible to advertisers' viral marketing campaigns that use technology to promote their products.

they spend isn't truly theirs," he writes, "they have no compelling reason to pay attention to how they spend it." Sounds sensible. But allowances in our house are modest; our children might say "stingy."

Owen offers some imaginative ideas for inspiring good financial behavior: Dad should create a fictitious bank with high interest rates (say, 3 percent a month) to teach children up to 12 the virtues of saving; Dad should create a fictitious stock market with shares valued at one hundredth of actual prices to teach teenagers the pleasures and perils of investing. I have done none of this.

As a journalist, I'm intrigued by the book's mere existence. It's more evidence of America's astounding affluence. The notion of lecturing children about mutual funds would have struck our ancestors as absurd. So, too, the possibility that children would have discretionary income. But they do. In 2002 all 12- to 19-year-olds spent $172 billion, estimates Teenage Research Unlimited. That was money under their control, not what parents spent on their behalf. It amounted to an average of $92 a week for 16- to 17-year-olds. An estimated 47 percent of these teens have cell phones.

Children are said to grow up faster now than ever before. In some ways, the opposite is true. A century ago many children—certainly those over 11 or 12—had jobs. On farms, many "worked as much as adults," notes sociologist Donald Hernandez of the State University of New York at Albany. As for factory work, the first child-labor law dates to 1837 in Massachusetts, reports economist Carolyn Moehling of Yale. By 1890, 17 states imposed age limits on hiring; three were as low as 10 and none higher than 14.

What made children work was not parental cruelty but economic necessity. Families needed labor and money. As economic creatures, children and teenagers have moved from being mainly workers to being mainly consumers. Of course, many teenagers have jobs today (about 40 percent of 16- to 19-year-olds are in the labor force). But their earnings go mainly for pocket money, not family income. A century ago teenagers started a life of full-time jobs; now most teens have part-time or temporary jobs.

U.S. Teen Spending* (in Billions), 2006 vs. 2011

2006 $189.7

Projected

2011 $208.7

*Products bought by and for teens

Taken from: Packaged Facts, "The Teens Market in the U.S." as cited in press release, June 26, 2007.

It wasn't until most teenagers were in high school and began "to look to one another and not to adults for advice, information, and approval" that they emerged as a distinct class, notes Grace Palladino, author of "Teenagers: An American History." This process culminated only in the 1950s. (In 1920, 16 percent of 17-year-olds were high-school graduates; by 1960 that was 63 percent.) But once it happened, aggressive advertisers and merchants responded.

Every young American now receives a free tutorial in envy and extravagance. This starts with a visit to Toys "R" Us and the endless aisles of dolls, videogames and sports equipment. After that it intensifies. On MTV, the program "Cribs"—my children actually like this (sob!)—features the homes of rich young rap stars, athletes and actors. Mercedeses, Hummers and Escalades crowd the garages; swimming pools and sculptures fill the backyards.

What fascinates me as a journalist baffles me as a parent. American culture creates a tension between achieving material success and not being controlled by it. How do we teach our children to use money wisely? I agree with Owen that we ought to provide guidance. But aside from parents' examples—our attitudes toward money, spending and saving—I am at a loss. I lack Owen's optimism that good financial judgment can by imbued by artificial games. Sensible saving and investing habits strike me as adult skills that must be mastered as adults. Even if I'm wrong, the stock market's collapse suggests that today's parents aren't the best teachers.

The trouble is that today's middle-class children are educated into a doctrine of effortless wealth. We parents may make it worse. The very comfort that we try to create for our children may give them the misleading impression that achieving the same for themselves will be more automatic than it is. As adults, my children won't be able to use money wisely unless they first earn it. I wish I had a formula for ensuring they'll get well-paid and satisfying jobs, but aside from the usual advice (work hard, follow your dreams, be lucky), I have none. This may be unavoidable, but I count it as another failure.

FOUR

Money Management Should Be Taught in Schools

Braun Mincher

In the following viewpoint financial writer Braun Mincher writes that the financial decisions that students will face in the future are far more complex than ever before. This, coupled with the fact that many young people are not financially literate, will lead to a generation that is not prepared to make difficult financial decisions, Mincher says. Financial literacy should be taught in schools, he argues, since it is just as relevant to real life—if not more—than other required subjects, like trigonometry and English. Mincher is the author of *The Secrets of Money: A Guide for Everyone on Personal Financial Literacy.*

Why does the school system require classes such as math, English, and science, but not basic personal finance?

We force students to learn trigonometry, yet how many of us ever use it again after graduation? In contrast, how many transactions involving money will we each conduct on a daily basis for the rest of our lives?

Think about each time you purchase something with a credit card, make a car payment, reconcile your bank account, or pay taxes. Even though these transactions are a daily occurrence for

Braun Mincher, "We Teach Teens Trigonometry, Why Not Money 101?" *Christian Science Monitor*, September 23, 2008. Reproduced by permission of the author.

Experts say that personal finance classes for teens, like this one in Chicago, are critical in preparing young people to make intelligent financial decisions.

most consumers, we receive very little financial education on them from our school system, or even our parents.

Now think about how huge a decision it is to rent or purchase a home, apply for a loan or mortgage, make a contribution to your IRA [individual retirement account] or 401(k) [employee- and employer-contributed retirement account], shop for insurance, or get married. How do we expect to make wise financial decisions when we have little education on even the basics?

According to a 2007 survey commissioned by the National Council on Economic Education, only seven states currently require high school students to receive financial education in the school system. What about the other 43 states?

We need look no further than the daily news headlines about the mortgage meltdown, the stock market crisis, the housing slump, or the rising cost of oil to see how relevant financial literacy is.

We Need to Educate Future Generations

Rather than waiting for the system to correct itself, we need to educate our future generations to make smarter financial decisions.

Just 20 years ago, personal finance was significantly less complex than it is today, and in many cases, parents supplemented what the schools did not teach.

Fast forward to present day, and we now have hundreds of different home mortgage options and the burden of retirement planning is shifting from the government and traditional company pension plans to consumers through investment vehicles such as IRAs and 401(k)s.

Because of their own financial woes, in many cases, parents are no longer comfortable with talking to their children about the touchy subject of money and personal finance.

Sadly, research shows that financial illiteracy has reached epidemic levels with no end in sight.

Much has been done to bring awareness to other growing crises such as childhood obesity, the need to wear sunscreen, and the dangers of drug and alcohol abuse, but why has something as important as financial literacy been largely ignored?

Results from my recent online consumer survey, Financial LiteracyQuiz.com, show that:

- Only 50 percent of those who took the survey know that property taxes and mortgage interest are tax deductible.
- Only 40 percent know that their liability for credit-card fraud is limited to $50.
- Only 33 percent know what "annual percentage rate" (APR) means.
- Only 32 percent know what required deductions are taken from their paycheck.

Are You Financially Literate?

1) Suppose you had one hundred dollars in a savings account, and the interest rate was 2 percent per year. After five years, how much do you think you would have in the account if you left the money to grow?

a) More than $102.00

b) Exactly $102.00

c) Less than $102.00

d) Do not know

2) Imagine that the interest rate on your savings account was 1 percent per year and inflation was 2 percent per year. After one year, would you be able to buy more than, exactly the same as, or less than today with the money in this account?

a) More than today

b) Exactly the same as today

c) Less than today

d) Do not know

3) Do you think that the following statement is true or false? "Buying a single company stock usually provides a safer return than a stock mutual fund."

a) True

b) False

c) Do not know

Answers:

1) a—More than $102; **2)** c—Less than today; **3)** b—False

Taken from: Annamaria Lusardi, "Are You Financially Literate? Do This Simple Test to Find Out," Financial Literacy and Ignorance, July 12, 2008. http://annalusardi.blogspot.com.

School Systems Have an Obligation to Prepare Students for the Global Economy

So, why should Americans care? These are basic pieces of information that are critical to financial decisions. And the better job we do of financially educating the next generation, the more financially independent they will be. This will not only mean breaking free from ongoing support from parents or destructive financial habits, but it could potentially save a lot of money.

Our school system has an obligation to prepare students for success in a fast paced global economy. Personal finance is a subject that will affect all consumers for the rest of their lives, regardless of age, education level, or income.

Financial literacy is a fundamental life skill that needs to be properly taught in the school system, alongside traditional math, English, and science.

The public needs to put pressure on lawmakers to mandate this. Parents and students need to be vocal locally.

In the meantime, consumers need to accept personal responsibility and invest in themselves to get financially educated. They can start by reading a book, attending a seminar, or getting coaching from a trusted adviser. But they have to start now. The future of our financial lives depends on it.

FIVE

Money Management Should Be Taught by Parents

Kimberly Palmer

> In the following selection Kimberly Palmer argues that the best course to reverse the "nationwide crisis in financial literacy" is for parents to teach their children about money management. She cites research showing that financial literacy programs in schools are not very effective and argues that parents are better equipped for the job. Parents have the opportunity to give children allowances, help their kids set financial goals, and talk about family money decisions. Palmer is a senior editor for *U.S. News & World Report* and writes about money management.

When I was just out of college, my mom wrote a letter to my younger sisters and me filled with financial lessons she had learned over the years. She explained how she and my dad had earned less than a combined $40,000 when they got married but managed to save $10,000 during that first year, which let them buy a small house. Eventually, their frugal ways helped them pay for all of our college tuitions. She recommended saving as much as possible, avoiding credit-card debt, budgeting, and diversifying investments.

My mom is hardly alone in trying to pass on financial know-how to her kids. In fact, teaching children about money is a growing concern among parents. And for good reason. Amid what could be considered a nationwide crisis in financial literacy, as illustrated by burgeoning consumer debt and paltry savings rates, parental guidance might be one of the few ways to reverse those trends.

Home study. It's also one of the most effective. While much research suggests that financial literacy programs in schools have little effect on students' later behavior, Lewis Mandell, a finance professor at the University of Washington, has found a strong connection between motivation and financial literacy. That suggests parents who persuade their kids that money management matters probably help them make smarter choices as adults. While Mandell recommends that teachers also promote motivation, he says that with such a personal and emotional subject, parents can probably better get through to their children.

Many parents, though, avoid the topic altogether. A recent Charles Schwab survey found that only 1 in 5 parents frequently

Many money management professionals say that parents should teach their children about handling personal finances, but a recent survey found that only one in five do.

Top Ten Vital Money Skills for Teens

• Balancing a checkbook	• Dealing with debt
• Budgeting money	• Paying taxes
• Financing college	• Considering all costs
• Establishing credit	• Saving for the future
• Identifying wants vs. needs	• Stretching a dollar

Taken from: Bankrate.com, MSN Money, "10 Vital Money Lessons for Teens," September 4, 2008. http://articles
.moneycentral.msn.com/CollegeAndFamily/RaiseKids/10-vital-money-lessons-for-teens.aspx?page=all.

involves teens in family budgeting and spending decisions. Just over half of parents teach their teens how to save on a regular basis. With the financial world increasingly complicated—many parents themselves may not understand the inner workings of credit cards and retirement accounts—kids can easily leave for college knowing less about financial matters than about their school meal plan.

Alarm over such ignorance has stimulated a handful of new ventures designed to help parents teach kids. Money Savvy Generation, a company cofounded by former financial services professional Susan Beacham, uses a piggy bank with four compartments—save, spend, donate, and invest—to teach kids how to budget. "You're teaching them to stop, pause, and reflect, and this is the first step toward teaching them to delay gratification," she says. Having everyone in the family, including adults, draw a picture of his or her goals, from pet gerbils to European vacations, also helps kids visualize the benefits of saving, Beacham adds.

Sometimes, starting that thought process can take less than 30 seconds. I recently overheard a teacher on a school field trip ask her student, who had expressed interest in a pricey car, "What job are you going to do so you can buy that car?"

Both Beacham and Mandell put their own children in charge of money from allowances or gifts so that they could learn how to take responsibility for it. "It's about teaching them a habit that will stick," says Beacham, whose teenage daughters purchased school lunches and clothing with their allowances. Mandell's daughter, now 35, learned to diversify investments when she purchased Pepsi stock and then watched it fall 40 percent.

Those hands-on lessons are powerful. While I had trouble recalling the specific points of my mom's letter until she recently re-sent it to me, I do remember when the technology mutual fund I purchased in the late 1990s plunged in price. I've kept my short-term savings in bonds ever since.

SIX

Credit Cards Teach Teens Money Management

Laura Rowley

> In the following viewpoint financial writer Laura Rowley says that credit cards can be a "potentially dangerous enemy" to teenagers and that, she argues, is exactly why teens should have one. Getting a card, she writes, will teach teens how to use credit responsibly. Rowley notes that teens who successfully handle credit cards can earn a good credit rating, plus take advantage of incentives like cash back and frequent-flyer miles. By contrast, she argues, teens who do not understand how to use credit may later find themselves saddled with late fees and high interest rates. Rowley is a journalist who specializes in personal finance and values. She is the author of *Money and Happiness: A Guide to Living the Good Life*.

A decade ago, when someone asked me if a high school student should have a credit card, my answer was a resounding "no." You might say I've made a 180-degree turn to the dark side.

No, I'm not getting paid by the credit card industry. I think those companies are a potentially dangerous enemy, and you have to prepare your child to be a worthy opponent in battle. You want them to conquer this prospective foe, and transform it into a humble servant that does their bidding.

Conquering the Conquerors

Plastic, for better or worse, has become ubiquitous. As I wrote in an earlier column, Chase Bank has been sending my kids—ages 4, nearly 8, and 10—credit card solicitations ever since I signed them up for a Continental frequent flyer program. This despite calls to the company asking it to stop.

So your kids have two options: 1) Become enslaved by late fees, finance charges, and high interest rates on mortgages and other loans, or 2) Conquer plastic and use it to build a stellar credit score, get cash back, and earn free travel perks. The sooner they understand their options, the better.

Think of credit cards as similar to online social networking—another phenomenon that didn't exist when I was a kid. Do I ban my kids from using the computer? Of course not; we discuss which sites are safe, which sites aren't, and why they should never give anyone personal information online.

Would You Give Your Teen His or Her Own Credit Card?

Number of parents	Responses	Percentage
724	Yes	23 percent
1,237	Yes, but one that I can control	40 percent
929	No way!	30 percent
153	Not sure	5 percent
3,043	Total Votes	

Taken from: "Would You Give Your Teen Their Own Credit Card?" About.com, January 14, 2008.
http://parentingteens.about.com/gi/pages/poll.htm?poll_id=1950094338&linkback=.

The College of Hard Knocks

If they aren't getting them already, teens will be inundated with credit card offers the second they set foot on a college campus, where they'll be urged to sign up in exchange for a T-shirt or Frisbee. According to a study by student loan firm Nellie Mae, the average college freshman has $1,500 in credit card debt, and that figure doubles by the time they graduate. Some 56 percent of college seniors carry four or more credit cards.

That's when the real trouble starts, because if teens lose the battle to understand and manage credit cards at 18, the damage can haunt them for years. An estimated 70 percent of employers check credit scores before they hire. Over time, a low credit score will suck tens of thousands of dollars out of your child's pocket when they seek financing for an auto or a home.

The damage is far more enduring than, say, flunking a college course—and yet kids get a heck of a lot more training in study habits. A 2007 survey on teens and money by Charles Schwab found just 30 percent said they think their parents are concerned with making sure they learn the basics of smart money management. Only one-quarter said they've learned how to use a credit card responsibly. And they crave parental guidance: Nearly two-thirds would rather learn through experience than in a classroom.

Half of teens agree it's easier to buy things with a credit card than with cash. Twenty-nine percent prefer to use plastic instead of cash, the study found. That's not the majority, but the number is skyrocketing: It jumped 61 percent between 2006 and 2007.

Prepaid Preparation

Start your teen off with a prepaid credit card. You can load the card with cash, and when it's gone, it's gone. Meanwhile, you can monitor where your teen is spending the money by tracking the card activity online.

The big drawback: Prepaid cards have a plethora of fees. First, consider the number of transactions you expect your teen to make each month. Some cards charge $1 to $2 per transaction, while others charge a flat monthly fee of a few dollars. You'll often pay

Some parents give their teens prepaid credit cards for necessities and as a means of teaching them personal financial responsibility.

to load money onto the card, as well as ATM fees of $1 to $2 on withdrawals. Your teen should check their balance online, because a balance request by ATM or phone will trigger another fee.

Look for a card with no overdraft fees, as these can add up quickly. And watch out for stupid fees: Some companies charge $150 to activate a card, and a customer service call to Valor Prepaid MasterCard costs 90 cents per minute.

Allowing Kids Big Buxx

Among the cards specifically marketed to teens, Visa Buxx and Allow MasterCard offer a fairly good package. Visa Buxx is the oldest player in the teen money field, and the cheapest upfront. It has no transaction fee or monthly maintenance fee; some banks that issue the card charge no load fee if you link the card to their checking account.

But watch out: Visa Buxx hits you with an overdraft fee (Wachovia's is $20 per overdraft). Teens learning to manage money could run that up pretty quickly.

Allow MasterCard is more expensive—about $45 in startup fees and a flat $3.50 monthly fee. But there are no overdraft fees, and the card can be loaded for 75 cents if linked to a checking account. Allow also offers 35 nifty automated controls, so parents can limit the amount spent per week, the amount spent at any one merchant, and so on. For instance, a parent can load $100 at the beginning of the month and limit the spending to $25 a week. (This helps save on loading fees.)

You're the Role Model

A survey conducted by Allow found that by the end of the month, 95 percent of parents had no idea how much they had given their children to spend, says Tom Smith, who founded the Arizona-based company two years ago.

"It's 'ask and you shall receive'—lunch money, haircuts, tennis shoes," says Smith. "If parents don't know how much they give kids, how do they learn to be accountable?" Smith gave each of his two granddaughters, ages 12 and 13, a card with $50 a month on it—but the kids have to manage their funds and cover the $3.50 monthly fee from their budget, or they lose the card.

Once your kid gets the hang of the prepaid card, you can switch to a grownup version that has fewer bothersome fees. Of course, that means you need to be modeling the behavior you'd like to see, by paying off your own credit cards on time and in full every month. You can't prepare your child for battle if you're sleeping with the enemy.

SEVEN

Teens Should Not Have Credit Cards

Janet Bodnar

In the following selection Janet Bodnar argues that giving teens credit cards is not the best way to teach them about credit. Bodnar writes that the best way to teach teens about credit is to have them use cash. She points out that prepaid cards that are aimed at children are little more than marketing gimmicks loaded with fees. Bodnar also advises parents to discuss credit card debt and the time it takes to pay off that debt using some type of interactive example instead of just lecturing. Bodnar is the editor of *Kiplinger's Personal Finance* magazine.

Not long ago, I was asked to appear on a TV show to discuss whether youngsters should carry credit cards. "What's to discuss?" I asked the producer. "That's the dumbest idea I've ever heard." Not so fast, I was told. Some people think that if kids use credit cards when they're still at home, they will handle credit responsibly when they're on their own.

I repeat: It's the dumbest idea I've ever heard. Giving your kids credit cards is like letting them use drugs early so that they won't turn into addicts. I'm all for learning to use credit responsibly, but a card to practice on isn't the way to do it.

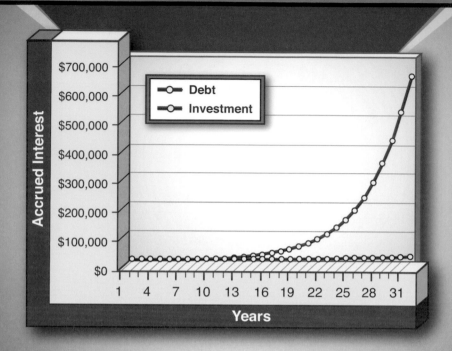

Investing $1,000 at 10 Percent Interest vs. Carrying $1,000 of Credit Card Debt at 23.99 Percent Interest

Taken from: "How Credit Cards Try to Keep You in Debt for Life," HugeDebt.com, October 11, 2006. www.hugedebt.com/credit-strategies.php.

The best way to teach kids to manage credit is to have them start with cold, hard cash—cold and hard being the operative words. Spending money is more real to kids, even teenagers, when they have to count out the bills and look down into an empty wallet. As my 16-year-old son puts it, "If I don't have cash, I can't buy stuff I don't need. If have a credit card, I can buy anything."

Magic Money

That's what makes a new marketing gimmick like the Hello Kitty Debit MasterCard so insidious. Like the Visa Buxx card, which has been around a while, Hello Kitty is a prepaid card aimed at children. Parents are encouraged to get the card for girls as young as 10 and reload it with cash when it's empty. The card, which is also loaded with fees, can be used to make purchases or get cash out of an ATM. Purchases can be tracked online, and pushers of this plastic promote it as a way to help kids learn to manage finances.

But kids won't get it. To them, plastic is magic money. Credit cards, debit cards, prepaid cards—you name it, they're all just a direct line to Mom and Dad's wallet. In one survey, 35% of teens said having a prepaid cash card would make them "look cooler in front of their friends."

What card issuers really want to do is get plastic into little hands so kids can buy stuff, online and elsewhere (Hello Kitty bills itself as the "cutest way to shop"). To get Moms and Dads to

Credit card companies run promotions that are specifically designed to entice teenagers into getting credit cards.

buy into this, one of the creators of the Hello Kitty card told the *Washington Post* that parents can monitor where their daughters spend money: "You get a higher level of control than if you just gave your daughter $100 and said, 'Go to the mall.'"

But parents have even more control if they insist their children finance mall excursions out of their own earnings or allowance, which I define as a fixed amount of money that kids get at regular intervals to pay for agreed-upon expenses. I've got nothing against kids buying stuff—as long as they don't hit up their parents for $20 to $100 every time they head out the door.

Life Lessons

That's not to say you shouldn't discuss credit with high schoolers. But instead of lecturing them, use a quick, interactive example, such as an online calculator to show them how long it can take to pay off a credit-card bill.

Once teens have learned to handle cash, they can start to use plastic in ways that make sense. For example, when they get a part-time job, help them open a checking account with an ATM or debit card so they can deposit, withdraw and spend their own money.

College students don't need credit cards, either. "I had a gasoline card for emergencies," one young woman confessed, "and my roommate and I always used it to buy food at the gas-station convenience store." The time to apply for credit is shortly before they graduate, after they've had experience managing money for several years and can appreciate the distinctions among the various cards. When I recently drove my college-senior son back to school, he and I had a long talk about when to use a credit versus a debit card—a discussion my 16-year-old would not have the patience for.

EIGHT

Prepaid Credit Cards Teach Money Management

Steve Brown

In this selection Steve Brown notes the problems Americans are having with credit card debt and makes the case that prepaid credit cards are a safe alternative, particularly for teens. He details the advantages of such cards, including the ease of getting them, the lack of interest and not having the danger of going into debt. He notes some disadvantages as well, but concludes that the safety, convenience and lack of debt on prepaid cards make them a good bet. Brown is the owner of American Cyberspace, a company that owns and manages Web sites, including several about credit cards and prepaid cards.

A ccording to a recent Experian-Gallup poll, 31 percent of Americans are having trouble making ends meet, and 49 percent of American consumers don't pay their credit card balance in full at the end of the month. Many hardworking, middle-class Americans are struggling with their finances, and credit card debt is playing no small part in the decline of the American standard of living. One smart way to avoid credit card debt and credit card interest charges: use prepaid credit cards, also known as prepaid debit cards or stored value cards.

Steve Brown, "Prepaid Credit Cards: A Great Payment Option for Both Mature Adults and Teens," www.debthelp.tv, June 7, 2008. Reproduced by permission of the author.

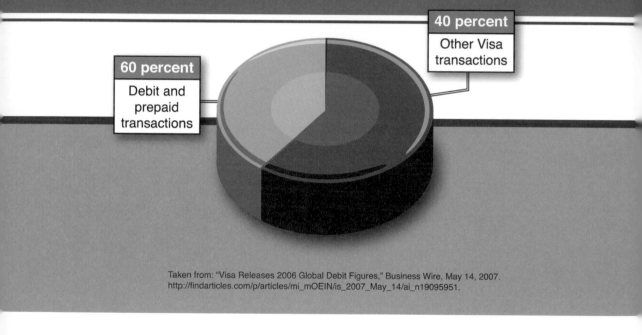

Visa Transactions in 2006
(Total: 59 Billion)

On May 14, 2007, Visa International announced that total volume for Visa consumer debit and prepaid programs, including cash transactions, grew by 17.0 percent in 2006, reaching US$2.68 trillion. This compares with a total volume of US$2.29 trillion for the same period in 2005. Debit and prepaid now account for 60 percent of Visa global total consumer volume and over 67 percent of the number of Visa transactions, based on total consumer volume of US$4.4 trillion and 59.9 billion total transactions.

40 percent
Other Visa transactions

60 percent
Debit and prepaid transactions

Taken from: "Visa Releases 2006 Global Debit Figures," Business Wire, May 14, 2007. http://findarticles.com/p/articles/mi_mOEIN/is_2007_May_14/ai_n19095951.

Prepaid credit cards work the same way traditional credit cards do and can be used to pay for all manner of goods and services at virtually any place that accepts regular credit cards. The main difference between a prepaid card and a regular credit card is that with a prepaid card you need to fund the account before making purchases. And since you don't work with a credit line with prepaid cards, they are ideal for people who want to enjoy the benefits of owning a Visa® or MasterCard®, but who also don't want to shoulder the burden of credit card debt and credit card interest charges.

Advantages of Prepaid Credit Cards

- Prepaid credit cards are much easier to get than standard credit cards. Just about anyone and everyone who applies for a prepaid card gets their application accepted. You can even order a prepaid credit card online from the convenience of your home. There are no credit checks or minimum income requirements.
- When using a prepaid card to pay for goods and services, you don't have to worry about amassing debt. You simply fund your prepaid card, spend the money at your leisure, then fill the card up again.
- With prepaid credit cards, you don't pay any interest as a result of making purchases. With a standard credit card, interest charges can accumulate rapidly, especially if the credit card in question engages in the practice of double-cycle billing.
- Prepaid credit cards don't charge annual, late payment or over-the-limit fees that often accompany standard credit cards.
- A parent can give a teenaged child a prepaid credit card to use for college spending. Giving a college student a prepaid card as opposed to a regular card has its advantages, the most salient being that a student can learn how to control his or her spending—a critical life lesson—without losing sleep worrying about fees, interest charges or the dreaded situation of having credit card debt at an early age.
- In general, prepaid credit cards provide the same fraud protection that regular credit cards offer. If you own a prepaid credit card with fraud protection, you can, in most circumstances, have charges that you didn't make refunded back to your card.

Disadvantages of Prepaid Credit Cards

- The vast majority of prepaid cards require you to pay a setup or activation fee when you first open a prepaid credit card account. The setup fee is usually nominal—typically between $5 and $20—and it varies from one card to another, but it can be as high as fifty dollars. This may seem like a lot, but remember that it's a one-time charge, and when you compare this to the fees associated with regular credit cards, a one-time setup fee really isn't that burdensome. Certain prepaid cards also charge a monthly maintenance fee.

- Another drawback to prepaid credit cards is that you might not be able to use them when setting up automatic billing (e.g. having your local utility company automatically charge you for your electricity usage each month).
- When using a prepaid credit card, no activity reports are made to the three major credit bureaus (TransUnion, Experian and Equifax). This means that transactions made using a prepaid card will not affect your credit history. This can be considered either an advantage or a disadvantage, depending upon your spending, budgetary and payment habits. If you are the type of

A young girl uses a prepaid credit card to purchase items online.

person who misses a credit card payment every once in a while, then using a prepaid card for your spending would probably be advantageous for you, since you wouldn't have to worry about a missed payment being reported to the credit bureaus. On the other hand, if you are trying to improve you credit score and you are very disciplined about making timely payments to your creditors, then you'd probably be better off getting a standard credit card with the best possible terms and conditions.

Prepaid credit cards have been gaining in popularity in recent years, and are likely to continue doing so. A standard credit card is a great financial tool when used responsibly, but standard cards aren't for everyone. Bottom line: prepaid cards are a safe, convenient and debt-free payment alternative for all types of consumers.

NINE

Prepaid Credit Cards Are Not a Cure-All

Jonathan Chevreau

In the following viewpoint Jonathan Chevreau calls prepaid credit cards "among the more insidious ways lenders have devised to get consumers to spend more." He agrees that the cards can be convenient but warns that the cards come with extra costs, including withdrawal fees, reloading charges and membership fees. Plus, he adds, the cards are often more difficult to use than regular credit cards and may require preauthorization for certain transactions. Chevreau writes "The Wealthy Boomer" column for the Canadian publication *The Financial Post*.

Among the more insidious ways lenders have devised to get consumers to spend more is the prepaid credit card.

These look like ordinary credit cards but are preloaded with a certain amount of cash up front. There are no interest charges, so there's no way of spending more than the preloaded amount.

But like other aspects of a cashless society, the convenience of these cards comes at a price—yearly membership fees, "reloading" fees and still more fees to make withdrawals from automated teller machines.

Prepaid credit cards have a five-year head start in the United States because 60 million Americans have no access to normal banking services, says David Eason, CEO [chief executive officer] of Toronto-based Berkeley Payment Solutions. As well, 10,000 U.S. financial institutions can issue Visa or Mastercards versus just 17 in Canada.

One of the earliest entrants in Canada was credit union Van City. Its prepaid Visa cards can be loaded with $25 to $500 worth

Projected Growth of Prepaid Credit Cards in the United States

Number and Value of Branded and Private Label Prepaid Card Transactions

Taken from: "Prepaid Cards: The State of the Industry," Aite Group, July 2007.
http://aitegroup.com/reports/figures/200707231-1.png.

of buying power. Announced in November, 2005, they were hailed as being "just in time for Christmas." Claiming a first in Canada, Van City said at the time the Canadian prepaid credit card market could be worth $2.4-billion.

The Youth Market

One successful niche is the youth market, notably the MuchMusic Prepaid Mastercard, launched in March, 2007. These cards can be handy helping kids make online purchases or helping parents dole out money (and monitor purchases) while their children are travelling or at college.

Maybe too handy, given how much time modern teens spend on the Internet. Promoters claim prepaid credit cards help teens learn the basics of budgeting and financial management. Critics see them as a way to hook them on real credit cards.

MuchMusic's Web site says prepaid credit cards are not actually credit cards, "so you don't have to worry about getting carried away with your spending." Because the numbers on the card are not embossed, they can't even be used on old-fashioned imprint machines in stores. Children ages 13 to 15 can get the card if they specify their parents as account holders; those 16 or older can apply for their own.

Fees and Charges

There are no monthly fees, but the first-year "membership and activation fee" is $34.95 and MuchMusic dings you another $9.95 in year two. Unlike some rivals, there is no purchase fee each time the card is used but it costs $1.50 to load on more cash. There's also a $1 charge to withdraw cash from ATMs, above and beyond what the ATM owner charges. If the card expires, an inactive fee of $2 a month is charged against any funds remaining.

Nor is using it as simple as it may appear. Preauthorization may be required for hotel reservations or car rentals. MuchMusic notes the amounts of preauthorized transactions at restaurants or gas stations may vary from actual purchases, with the correct amounts not apparent until the transaction history is mailed out.

Why Not Just Use Debit Cards?

If they are merely glorified debit cards, why not bypass the fees and use real debit cards? I'd argue a teenager would be better off with a regular debit card that can be regularly reloaded for nothing through the simple expedient of holding down a part-time job and having the paycheque deposited automatically into their account.

Youth marketing expert Max Valiquette, president of Toronto's Youthography, says prepaid credit cards are "pseudo credit cards" that are priming kids to make the jump to real credit cards. However, he defends their use in some situations. Many teens want to purchase items like concert tickets online and can't do so with debit cards, he says. They can download music from services like Apple's iTunes, but must use real credit cards. Valiquette thinks prepaid cards are safer in these situations than real credit cards.

Critics say that prepaid credit cards are a means to hook teenagers on real credit cards.

Credit Canada executive director Laurie Campbell says anything promoting credit card–like products to teens is potentially dangerous. "In Canada, we have such a lack of education on the wise use of credit that even though these cards are prepaid, it is assuredly an avenue into the world of regular credit cards once they come of age."

Companies Looking to Make Money on the Cards

If prepaid credit cards aren't yet ubiquitous, it's because their economics are less compelling for financial institutions. They can't make the big bucks charging high interest rates on unpaid balances so they have to make it up in fees. Some banks don't want to be perceived as gouging consumers on these fees, says Berkeley's Eason. "They want to make sure the cards have a strong value proposition for consumers."

He sees more potential on the corporate side, which is why Berkeley and Scotiabank just announced the first corporate prepaid Visa cards in Canada. These corporate incentive prepaid cards help firms extend their brands, boost employee morale or customer loyalty and may even help them tap new markets. Eason says the prepaid card is less costly to issue than cheques or merchandise and companies are discovering its significant value as a marketing tool by showcasing their name or logo on each card.

TEN

Credit Card Companies Push Teens into Debt

Megan McWethy

> In the following selection Megan McWethy writes that
> students are getting credit cards in their teens and accu-
> mulating too much debt as a result. The credit card com-
> panies target college students and have been successful
> in making profits off the debts carried by the students.
> McWethy notes that most students pay only the min-
> imum balance each month, which results in the debt
> taking years to be paid off. McWethy was the lifestyles
> editor at *The Arkansas Traveler* when this article was
> written.

The flyer reads, "Free 10" 1 Topping Pizza & Drink!!!" in big,
bold letters, and the students being handed the yellow slips of
paper are excited that for tonight, dinner is no longer a concern.

But underneath the heading that promises pepperoni pies is a
much smaller type: "Must participate in student promo."

The offer is that in exchange for a small pizza, students must
first sign up for a credit card. A few forms, questions and signatures
later they are walking out the door, cardboard box in hand.

But with today's student in credit card debt for thousands of
dollars, the trade-off might not be such a good deal.

Megan McWethy, "Student Credit Card Debt in the Thousands," The Arkansas Traveler Online,
January 17, 2006. Copyright © 2006 The Traveler. Reproduced by permission.

Teens' Top Five Places to Shop

1). **Hollister**

2). **American Eagle Outfitters**

3). **West Coast Brands** (including Billabong, Roxy, and Volcom)

4). **Abercrombie & Fitch**

5). **Forever 21**

Taken from: "Taking Stock with Teens," Piper Jaffray, April 10, 2007.

An Alarming Trend

"The average college student caries between $3 and $7,000 in credit card debt," UA [University of Arkansas] Finance Instructor John Rownak said, "and the typical graduate student now has over $20,000 of combined student loan and credit card debt."

The alarming trend is one that is familiar to former UA student Dustin Terrell. After racking up almost $10,000 in credit card debt, he found himself in a desperate situation.

"At first I said [my credit card] was just for special occasions, but it was easier to just put the charge on there when I didn't have money and say 'oh I'll just pay it off later,'" he said.

Students like Terrell, who got his first credit card at 19, are obtaining cards when they are still in their teens and this can help motivate spending and eventually debt.

"There's no question [students] are getting credit cards at an earlier age," said Rownak, who teaches Personal Financial Management. "My class is junior level and virtually all the students in my class have at least one credit card and over half have more than one."

A recent article in *USA Today* stated that 23 percent of college students have gotten credit cards before they entered college, said Joel Doelger, Director of Counseling for Credit Counseling of Arkansas. Debt from those cards can begin to accumulate as early as freshman year because when students enter college, they are targeted by credit card companies as potential new customers.

"Credit card companies have been successful in making good profits off of credit cards carried by college students and as a result, they are doing many more solicitations among college students now," Rownak said.

And the strategy works. According to a 2003 CBS News article, students double their credit card debt and triple the number of cards in their wallets between the time they arrive on campus and graduation.

The Consequences of Paying the Minimum

A big problem that many students, and other Americans, have is that they only pay the minimum amount due each month. With the average annual percentage rate at 13.37 percent, according to ABC News, it can take students years to pay off their debt.

"If they accumulate only $2,000 of credit card debt each year they were in college and had an $8,000 credit card balance when they graduated, and they made the minimum payment on the credit card, it would take them over 44 years to pay off that credit card," Rownak said. "They would pay over $20,000 in interest."

Terrell said he thinks students aren't aware of the consequences of paying only the minimum amount each month.

"Most don't realize you have to pay more than the bill; you have to pay the fees you tack on, too," he said. "You'll end up paying off your principal but you still have fees and the interest on your fees."

Doelger agreed with Terrell.

"You don't want to play the game of making just minimum payments on credit cards," said Doelger, who estimates that 5 to 8 percent of his clients are students. "It's a losing game."

With credit card offers at every corner, it can be hard to say no to credit card debt.

"I get a credit card solicitation in the mail everyday," Rownak said. "In a four-and-a-half month period, without [counting companies twice], I could have applied for over $200,000 in credit card debt. If I had done that, it would have taken forever to pay it off. The credit card companies know they'll have success based on the number of solicitations sent out."

As new spenders, teens often buy more than they need and inevitably end up with financial problems.

Using Credit Is Easy, Paying It Back Is Hard

The companies who send out credit card offers make it look simple to maintain a healthy financial history, Doelger said.

"They make it look so easy and using credit is easy, it's paying it back that's hard."

Terrell said he never realized how easy it was to fall in the credit card trap.

"Getting into debt is easier than what you think." He had 10 credit cards before he tossed them all and signed up for credit counseling at CCOA [Credit Counseling of Arkansas].

"I wised up to the fact that they weren't good for me," he said. "I'll never own one again and if I need credit, I'd rather have my parents co-sign a loan from a bank and pay that loan back to build credit.

"Always listen to people who have experience about it in the past; people who tell you not to get [credit cards], there's a reason for that."

But having a credit card isn't always a negative thing. Besides helping to build credit, charge cards are convenient as well: they can be used to purchase a car, or a good health insurance plan and make the process of finding an apartment that much easier, as they are used for deposits and rent payments. Credit cards are also useful in fronting large amounts of money in the cases of unexpected doctor bills or they can help save time by allowing the user to pay his monthly bills online.

"Credit cards have become a necessity," Rownak said. "It provides a student the ability to take advantage of an opportunity.

"You can't rent a car without a credit card, you can't purchase things over the Internet without a credit card," he said.

"There are a lot of reasons you need a credit card, you just have to have the discipline to use it for the right reason. Credit cards enable students and adults to get into trouble, but it's really up to us as individuals to use credit cards for the right reasons."

ELEVEN

Parents Spoil Kids by Giving Them Money

Jean Chatzky

In the following essay Jean Chatzky argues that parents should not be "walking ATMs." By not buying their kids whatever they want, parents are actually teaching valuable money lessons. According to Chatzky, when parents do not buy their children certain items, they are teaching what the family values. Even a disappointed child is good, she writes, since someone who learns to deal with disappointment at an early age will be better prepared to handle bigger disappointments later in life. Chatzky is the personal finance editor for the *Today Show*, editor-at-large for *Money* magazine and author of *Pay It Down! From Debt to Wealth on $10 a Day*.

Are we raising a generation of spoiled children? As a mother, it's a question I ask often and a topic I've debated more than a few times with friends.

I've seen teenagers with cell phones so high-tech I can't begin to understand them and cars twice as nice as mine. The new iPhone has become the ultimate status symbol not for just the 20-something crowd but for tweens and teenagers as well.

"Parenting has become a competitive sport. Parents are traveling over each other in an attempt to do what they think is better parenting, but in some instances, it's actually backfiring," says Dr. Gail Saltz, a Manhattan psychiatrist, best-selling author, *TODAY Show* expert and (full-disclosure) one of the friends with whom I've had those aforementioned debates. If your children have everything handed to them from an early age, not only will they struggle to care for themselves one day, but you'll also rob them of the satisfaction that comes from, say, finally getting that brand-new car you worked hard for.

We don't set out to spoil our children. Many of us simply want to give them the things we didn't have growing up, and that's

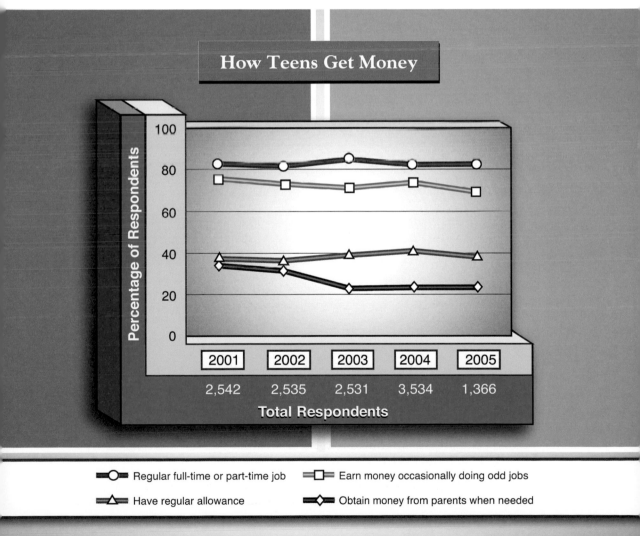

How Teens Get Money

Percentage of Respondents

| | 2001 | 2002 | 2003 | 2004 | 2005 |

Total Respondents: 2,542 2,535 2,531 3,534 1,366

⬤ Regular full-time or part-time job ◻ Earn money occasionally doing odd jobs
△ Have regular allowance ◇ Obtain money from parents when needed

Taken from: International Communications Research, August 2005.

understandable. I'm all for kids' having cell phones in case of an emergency. I'm against an automatic upgrade every time a new model hits the shelves. Children need to know that their belongings are valuable, not disposable. But how do you teach them this and other important lessons about money?

Walk the Walk

If you don't have control of your own money, you're well on your way to raising a child who behaves exactly the same way. And why shouldn't he? Children are innately observant and easily pick up our bad habits, whether that means one too many shopping sprees or a bounced check here and there.

"At the end of the day, children look to you because you're their model, and they'll emulate you, whether that's good or bad. If you're always struggling for the next big thing and living outside your means, they're not going to buy it when you try to teach them to do otherwise," Saltz explains. The best example you can possibly set is one of confidence, in both your finances and your lifestyle. No child needs to watch you max out a credit card in an effort to keep up with the Joneses.

Teens Need to Make Choices

One of the most important lessons when it comes to managing your money is that you can't have everything you want. It sounds pretty simple, but for many people, it's not—as evidenced by the soaring debt in this country. It's an even harder concept for your children to understand, but the easiest way to drive home the point is to stop bailing them out. Give them a set allowance (to hammer out an amount, get an idea of what the neighborhood parents are giving, then raise it a bit each year), and then show them how to budget so the money stretches out over an entire week.

If they screw up one week and blow all the cash on Monday, keep your wallet closed so they learn not to do it again. If you hand over more money, the only thing you'll teach them is to turn to you every time they're short on cash. And with 65 percent of

For a teenager the most important lesson in money management is that you can't always get what you want.

kids ending up back home after college, that's not a lesson you want to impart.

Sounds harsh, I know. But no matter how hard you work to shelter your kids, eventually, they're going to come across a bump or two. Teach them at an early age how to cope with a small disappointment here and there, and they'll have an easier time when the bumps turn into hills and mountains later in life. Believe it or not, denying a couple of requests for a candy bar over the years really might help your child when a job interview doesn't go well, or he doesn't get accepted to that Ivy League school.

"You really can impact your kid's ability to cope later on in life, take trauma and bounce back. If you never test that, and life is just on a big puffy cloud, they'll never build that skill and will really struggle as adults," Saltz says. So rest assured that it's OK to say no once in a while, if only because you said so.

As far as conversation topics go, money is right up there with sex. It's taboo, and a lot of families just don't talk about it. But if your children are asking for something that you just aren't ready to lay out the cash for, it's perfectly fine to say that. Then express your reasons—it's not in the budget right now, or spending the money on something else will bring more value to the family—without piling on too much information. This is where it tends to get tricky because it's important to strike a balance between explaining that the purchase isn't in the budget and needlessly burdening them with your financial problems.

In general, children will let you know what they're ready to hear about simply by asking, so if you stick to answering their direct questions, you'll usually come out fine.

Emphasize the Family's Values

It happens all the time: You tell your daughter she can't have the new dress she wants, but you're happy to write out a check in the same amount for piano lessons each month. Understandably, this can seem a bit contradictory to a kid, so use it as a lesson in what's important in your house. Sit down and explain why you spend money on some things, and not on others. Whether your focus is music, education or sports, explaining your family's individual values will help children understand your spending habits.

It can also help bail you out when the next-door neighbor gets the newest video game, and your son doesn't.

TWELVE

Teens Deserve Bigger Allowances

Yoni Goldstein

> Yoni Goldstein was inspired to write the following essay
> after seeing a 2007 study showing that teens in England
> get an average allowance of one thousand pounds—or
> about two thousand dollars—a year. Although some were
> upset by the high figure, Goldstein argues that such a
> large amount is necessary for today's teens. After all, he
> writes, with parents largely absent from the home, kids
> are responsible for entertaining themselves. In a way, the
> larger allowances are an acknowledgment—Goldstein
> calls it a "payoff"—from parents that they are not as
> available as they could be to their children. Goldstein is
> a writer for *The National Post*.

Here's what we know about the life of a typical teenager back
in the 1950s (note: Not being old enough to know what
family life was actually like 50 years ago, I've relied on reruns of
black-and-white TV episodes as my source): Mom was smiling
when you walked through the door from school, waiting with a
tray of milk and cookies. Supper was cooking in the oven and
dad was on his way home. On the weekend, you took your sweet-
heart to the drive-in, grabbed some chow and a root beer at the

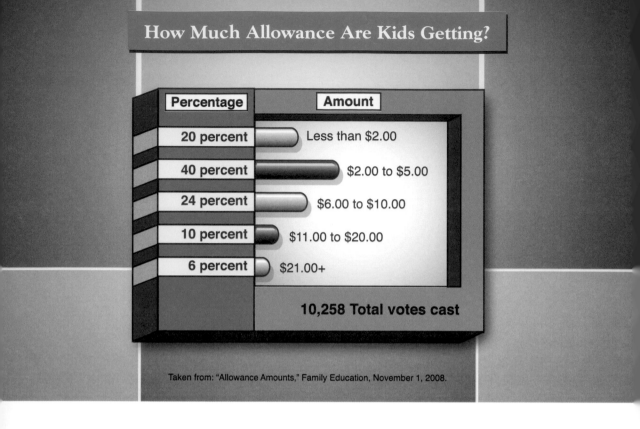

How Much Allowance Are Kids Getting?

Percentage	Amount
20 percent	Less than $2.00
40 percent	$2.00 to $5.00
24 percent	$6.00 to $10.00
10 percent	$11.00 to $20.00
6 percent	$21.00+

10,258 Total votes cast

Taken from: "Allowance Amounts," Family Education, November 1, 2008.

soda shop and, maybe, stopped by the secluded "lookout cove" that every city and town had back then. All before ending the night early and getting tucked in by midnight (at which point, dad put his arm around mom and said how great the kids were, even if they did get into a little trouble every now and then). Life couldn't have been better.

But, inevitably, all kids hear from their parents is how tough their teenage years were. Chores to do. Responsibilities. Toil. No Internet or 500 digital channels to surf through for entertainment. No cell phones or instant messaging or iPods. Life was hard—kids, the now-parents remind their kids, used to walk 20 kilometres to and from school, uphill both ways, et cetera, et cetera.

Plus, the elderly note, kids used to have to work for their own spending money—on the farm, at the grocery store or delivering papers. There was no allowance. Or, if there was, it was just a few pennies—enough to buy a chocolate bar or pack of hockey cards at the end of the week.

Old-timers employ a certain kind of selective memory when it comes to comparing their childhoods with those of current-day teenagers. That's why people are howling about a new survey out of England which reports that the average Brit teenager receives 1,000 pounds—about $2,000—annually in allowance money. "Kids have too much freedom," they say, "too many advantages." Were they to remember more closely, they would see that rising allowances correspond to the neglect of ever-less parent-like parents.

A survey reveals that teens in Britain receive almost $2,000 dollars a year in allowance money, in part because many parents feel guilty about not spending enough time with them.

Teen Life Is Different than Before

Sure, two grand is a lot of money for a 12- or 15-year-old to be walking around with. It's true that teenagers tend to not be the most wise of money spenders and, yes, a $2,000 allowance constitutes a mini-inheritance, not pocket change. But kids have it hard these days—much harder than the former teenagers who've turned into their 40- and 50-year-old parents ever did. They deserve a raise.

Consider: Nowadays, when kids get home from school there's no beaming mom to hand out cookies. More likely, there's a voice mail—worse yet, an e-mail—from mom, hurriedly saying she's stuck at work (and so is dad). There are leftovers in the fridge or a couple of bucks on the table in the hall to order some Chinese. And when they're not at work, mom and dad, who have become wealthier than their parents ever were for no reason other than the fact that everyone's gotten richer, like to go on vacation for a few days here and there or for dinner with friends or to see their favorite '80s hair band at the local arena. Work or play, the fact is parents aren't around for their kids the way they used to be.

Teenagers have been forced into the difficult task of entertaining themselves. And entertainment these days costs more than ever. A movie at the local giganta-plex costs $20 (with popcorn and drink), digital music downloads are cheaper than CDs but they ain't free—heck, even a chocolate bar or bag of chips costs $1.25. (Plus, according to the English survey, kids seem to need extra money to buy booze and cigarettes—both also more expensive than they used to be.) Worst of all, Lookout Cove, that final bastion of free (or at least cheap) entertainment, was long ago razed to make way for a new condo development.

Don't blame kids for their bloated allowances. Blame the parents who work too late, chase their own fancies too often and generally don't spend enough time with their kids. The extra allowance money is a payoff, an acknowledgement that family life isn't what it used to be. If it were, teenagers wouldn't need the money, and parents wouldn't need to hand it out.

THIRTEEN

Allowances Do Not Work

Liz Pulliam Weston

> In this selection, Liz Pulliam Weston argues that allowances do not work. Traditional weekly allowances in which parents give their kids a small amount of money each week do not teach crucial money management skills like budgeting, planning ahead, and making wise choices. In place of the usual weekly allowance, Weston advocates giving teens a lump sum of money to cover their expenses. This, she writes, provides real-world lessons in careful shopping, differentiating wants and needs, and living within one's means. Weston is a personal financial columnist for MSN Money, a syndicated columnist, and the author of the books *Easy Money: How to Simplify Your Finances and Get What You Want Out of Life* and *Deal with Your Debt*.

Raise your hand if any of the following sounds familiar:

- You give your children a weekly allowance, but they're constantly bugging you for more money or stuff.
- No matter how much you lecture about the importance of money and saving, cash just seems to slip through their hands.

- Deferred gratification, comparison shopping and the difference between wants and needs are all alien concepts to your kids. What matters is what their friends wear and have.
- You despair of your offspring ever having the financial skills needed to navigate adulthood successfully.

If this is the world you live in—or one you fear—it might be time to ditch the idea of an allowance altogether. Instead, consider replacing these weekly infusions with a monthly chunk of cash that your children use to cover most or all of their spending.

Instead of turning to you for clothing, school supplies and activity fees, your children manage those costs themselves—along with all their incidental expenses that used to be covered by their allowances.

Sound radical? It's obviously not an idea that could work for kids under 10. But neither is it a concept that should be delayed until college, which is when most young people get their first real crack at managing money, argues parent John Whitcomb.

Cash *and* Responsibility Can Work Wonders

By then, they'll be far from your supervision—and pelted with credit cards that can turn their bad spending habits into true financial disasters. Whitcomb, a Milwaukee, Wis., emergency room doctor and father of two, says it's much better to begin giving children the reins starting in middle school, while you're still able to supervise them.

Whitcomb outlined the concept in his book, *Capitate Your Kids*, also published as *The Sink or Swim Money Program*. Capitation is a health industry concept that basically means giving a fixed amount of money to doctors or a hospital to care for a population of patients. In essence, they're given both the money *and* the responsibility for spending it wisely.

Think how different that idea is from the traditional allowance. In most cases, an allowance is:

Too frequent. If you give your child money every week and she spends it all, she just has to wait a few days to get more.

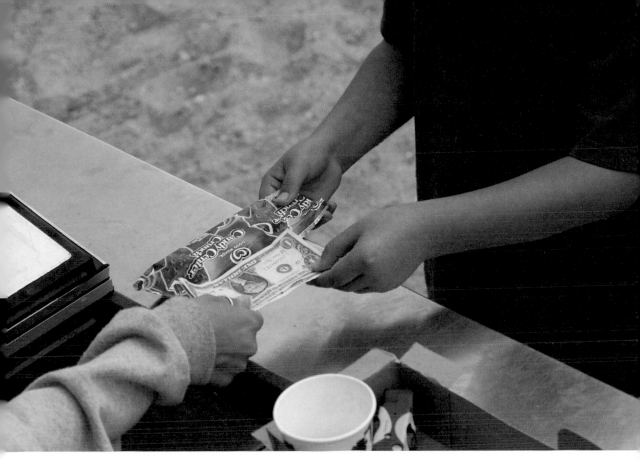

Teens whose parents give them large amounts of cash monthly, rather than a weekly allowance, may learn important concepts about managing their own finances.

There's little incentive to plan and not much real pain if she makes a mistake.

Not all-inclusive. Since you're still shelling out for most things, you remain the go-to person when your child wants something. That leads to nagging and whining—plus there's little opportunity for your child to learn true responsibility.

Too small. Allowances typically cover only discretionary expenses. In the adult world, however, most of our money goes to mandatory expenses—shelter, food, transportation, etc. Children need to learn the concept that most money is spoken for and not available for anything they want.

At the same time, kids who are given significant sums can learn some important concepts:

- Resources are finite.
- Longer-term planning is an important skill.
- Careful shopping can stretch what they have.

Once it's *their* money—to do with as they will—the choices they make tend to change.

Parent Rick Brohmer of Waukesha, Wis., has already noticed this phenomenon with his three older children, now grown. While they were in school, brand names were essential. As [they] left the nest and started buying on their own, brand names were less important, said Brohmer, who still has a 14-year-old, designer-desiring daughter at home.

Start with the Clothing Budget

John Whitcomb learned his own money skills as the child of missionary parents in India. Sent away to boarding school for four months at a stretch, he and his siblings were given a term's worth of cash at a time to pay their monthly tuition, buy clothes and cover their other expenses.

He adapted his experience into a six-step plan that starts when children are in middle school, with the creation and implementation of a clothing budget. Gradually, more expenses and responsibility are added. Kids learn to use an ATM card in ninth grade, a checkbook in 10th and a credit card in 11th to help manage their costs.

By the time they're ready for college, they're handling all their own expenses, including auto insurance and perhaps even paying their parents room and board.

Long-term saving, investing and charitable giving can be incorporated as priorities, as well.

You can start smaller, if you want. Some parents may find that a clothes budget may be too big for pre-teens to handle.

Screw-Ups Teach Great Lessons

Susan Beacham, a personal finance educator in suburban Chicago and co-founder of the Money Savvy Generation Web site, is starting her 12-year-old daughter Allison off with $25 a month to cover books, magazines and the once-a-month lunch out that her parents had been paying for.

Beacham and her daughter are still negotiating the details. Allison's not at all sure, her mom says, that the added responsibility is worth losing her mom as a source of constant funds.

She's still very apprehensive about taking it over, Beacham said. But we have to get more girls understanding that they have to grab the reins. It will help them in later life become the independent, risk-taking people we want them to be.

Parents who've tried capitation say screw-ups are inevitable— and an important part of the learning process. Nan Mead's sixth-grade son blew his first month's capital, meant to cover lunches, hair cuts and all his miscellaneous expenses, in a week on CDs and pizza for his friends. Mead, communications director for a financial education foundation in Colorado Springs, Colo., refused to give him more cash, and he wound up taking sack lunches to school. That was a big setback for a kid who thought hot lunches were cool. Gradually, he learned his lesson.

Big Enough Doses to Be Meaningful

His money management skills improved each month, Mead said. By Christmas, he was doing quite well, even saving for some short-term goals. Mead's son is now in college and handling money responsibly.

With their parents' help, kids on this plan learn to anticipate what expenses they'll face and how much they should set aside for them, Whitcomb said. They learn that, if they don't buy the $180 sneakers but settle for a $40 pair, they'll have more money for other things they want.

The parents have some work to do as well. They need to figure out how much is a reasonable amount for various expenses, and, almost invariably, they learn they're spending a lot more on their kids than even they suspected, he said.

But Whitcomb doesn't advise trying to save money by giving kids less than you'd spend otherwise. The idea isn't to cheap out but to teach children about money in big enough doses to be

A Sample Budget

Weekly Spending Evaluation

Weekly expenses

Food (lunch, snacks) _____

Public transportation (buses, subway) _____

Car (gas, upkeep, loan payments, insurance) _____

Entertainment (movies, games, magazines, CDs) _____

Computer (software, games, DVDs) _____

Communications (phone, cell phone, Internet service provider) _____

Gifts _____

Clothes _____

Savings _____

Total weekly expenses $ _____

Weekly income

Allowance _____

Earnings _____

Gifts _____

Other _____

Total weekly income $ _____

How did you do?

Total weekly income _____

Minus total weekly expenses − _____

The bottom line $ _____

What have I learned by tracking my spending?

_____

_____

_____

Taken from: "Talking to Teens About Money," Consumer Action, March 2, 2007.
www.consumer-action.org/english/articles/ talking_to_teens_about_money_en_2007.

meaningful—and for purposes that intensely interest them, he writes.

Your success comes not in saving money in the short term but in creating a state of mind that living contentedly within your means is the key to financial independence.

Monitor—but Resist the Urge to Rescue

Parents also need to keep tabs on their offspring's progress; Whitcomb recommends monthly meetings. He also believes parents should resist the urge to step in when their kids fail. If your kid does buy the more expensive sneakers but fails to save for the winter coat he needs, you shouldn't dig into your wallet, he says. You might, however, drive him to the nearest Salvation Army store.

Beacham says she's already learned that a firm but gentle hand pays dividends. On a recent shopping trip, her daughter began pleading for the latest issue of *Teen People*.

I said, "You've got your money; it's in your wallet. I reminded you to bring it," Beacham said. We walked out of that store with nothing.

As Allison gets used to handling money, she'll be given responsibility for more expenses. By the time she's a junior in high school, Beacham hopes to be giving her the money in one annual payout.

People are surprised by that, but, in two years, they'll be doing the same thing on a college campus, Beacham said, and they'll have seven credit cards.

FOURTEEN

Allowance Details Are Not as Important as the Lessons Learned

Gregory Karp

> Should allowances by tied to chores? Gregory Karp feels strongly that they should not, but argues in the following section that the question misses the bigger point. "The details of an allowance system aren't as important as making the effort to start one, adjusting it over time and teaching the lessons," he writes. Allowances are invaluable for teaching kids about spending, earning, saving, and giving. Karp recommends that parents let their kids make money mistakes. When children waste money and buy poor quality things, it is its own lesson. Karp is a personal finance writer for *The Allentown (PA) Morning Call* and author of *Living Rich by Spending Smart*.

Giving children an allowance is a topic that can befuddle even the most well-intentioned and well-informed parents. But the spending skills a child can learn from an allowance system far surpass the monetary value of the cash parents fork over to them.

As those children mature into adults, they will have to resist almost constant marketing pitches from advertisers on TV, Web sites, billboards, magazines and newspapers. And they'll probably have credit available to them, allowing them to buy even when they can't afford it.

Money troubles await children who don't learn that money is finite, and they have to make trade-off decisions with purchases. They'll have to distinguish between needs and wants. Many times a day, they'll need to tell themselves, "No."

Parents often have many questions: At what age do I begin giving an allowance? How much money should I give, and how often?

Chore and Allowance Statistics

Most Popular Chores Assigned

1. Make bed
2. Clean room
3. Feed pet

Highest Paying Chores

1. Mowing yard, $20 (highest amount paid)
2. Watch siblings, $15
3. Wash Car, $15

Lowest Paying Chores

1. Brush teeth, $.01
2. Lay out clothes for tomorrow, $.01
3. Do homework, $.01

Odd Chores and Statistics

1. Changing underwear pays $.05
2. Capping toothpaste pays $.02
3. Staying awake for sermons pays $.10
4. Waking up happy pays $.05

Taken from: "Chore and Allowance Statistics," PayJr., June 2007. www.payjr.com/education.html.

Should the child have to do household chores for the money? When do I raise the allowance? What spending or savings restrictions should I implement?

How Much to Give?

April is financial literacy month, so it is an appropriate time to think about giving an allowance. There are many allowance systems to consider. Below is a sample plan. You can modify it to fit your household.

How much? Beginning around the ages of 5 to 7, give 50 cents per week for each year old the child is. At age 10, give $1 per years old. A less accelerated plan is $1 weekly for each school grade level.

Customize amounts depending on what you can afford and what you think your child can handle. But don't give too little. The child needs to be able to save enough money in a relatively short period to buy something he or she actually wants.

Tied to chores? Don't confuse money lessons. Learning how to spend smart as a consumer is a different lesson from "you have to work for a living." You are not paying your children a salary; you're giving them money as a tool for learning, like you would give them a piano to practice on or flash cards with which to memorize multiplication tables.

So don't tie allowance to chores. Chores are to be done by the child for free because he or she is part of the household and has a responsibility to help operate it. If a child decides she doesn't feel like doing chores and will forgo the allowance, the allowance system crumbles and the lessons are lost. How will you respond when you tell her to make her bed and she asks, "How much are you going to pay me?"

To instill a work ethic and entrepreneurial spirit, offer a list of optional jobs a child can choose to complete for extra money.

Each Family Can Find Its Own System

If you disagree with this philosophy, go ahead and tie allowance to chores, but regularly talk to the child about both lessons separately—spending and earning.

Separating. Require the child to earmark money each pay period for three accounts: spending, saving and giving. For younger children, it's easy to place equal amounts into three containers or envelopes, labeled with each category. Identify types of purchases the child will be responsible for. Don't give loans or advances.

Spending. This account is where all the action is, and some of the best lessons. Money in this account should be spent regularly.

Allow children to make mistakes with this money. You want them to buy things impulsively that they later regret. You want them to buy a poor-quality item that breaks. You want them to run out of money, forcing them to save for several weeks to buy the next thing. You want them to choose among similar items with different prices.

Some experts say that allowances should be used by parents as a learning tool about managing money, rather than as a "salary" for doing chores.

Children need the repetition of buying things and witnessing the consequences of the decisions. Of course, parents should retain veto power over types of purchases, such as candy or dangerous toys.

Parents and Kids Should Talk About Money

Regularly talking to children after money decisions, especially poor spending decisions, is crucial. Talk about your own money life, too, such as why you're using coupons at the supermarket, how to fill out a check, how credit cards work.

Saving. The point of this account is to show how money adds up over time. This money is not to be spent but to be counted and monitored. When you dismantle the allowance system in the child's late teens, the money can be used for college expenses or a car, for example.

Giving. Earmarking money for weekly church donations or periodic donations to a charity provide a deeper lesson about what money can be used for.

Customizing. Adjust the allowance plan to fit lessons you are trying to teach. For example, include lunch money in older children's allowance and offer a deal: The children can keep the lunch money for each day they make a lunch at home and brown-bag it.

Or make your son or daughter responsible for their own back-to-school or holiday shopping. Switch to a monthly allowance for older children, forcing them to budget their money over a longer period. Make saving optional but offer to match the child's contribution to their savings dollar for dollar. Help a child sell an unwanted video game online to raise money for a new game.

The details of an allowance system aren't as important as making the effort to start one, adjusting it over time and teaching the lessons.

FIFTEEN

Jobs Help Teens Learn Money Management

Eve Tahmincioglu

> In the following viewpoint Eve Tahmincioglu cites a study showing that fewer teens are working for money. These kids who do not work, she argues, are missing out on valuable life lessons. Tahmincioglu points to a study showing that young adults who had held jobs in their teens had better interpersonal skills and confidence than those who did not work. Kids who work, she argues, also learn that money comes from toil, not from parental handouts. Tahmincioglu is the author of *From the Sandbox to the Corner Office: Lessons Learned on the Journey to the Top* and a columnist for MSNBC.com.

Teenagers are working their tails off in school and at everything from violin lessons to swim team, but fewer are working for the money these days, and that means they're missing out on a key rite of passage.

Witness Tim McBride, 16. The last thing he's thinking of is making minimum wage flipping burgers. As a sophomore majoring in cinematic studies at the Cab Calloway School of the Arts in Wilmington, Del., he has already made a prize-winning documentary chronicling the state insurance commissioner's

Who Is Making Minimum Wage?

Employed wage and salary workers paid hourly rates with earnings at or below the prevailing federal minimum wage by age, 2007 annual averages:

| Age | Total paid hourly rates | Number of workers (in thousands) | | |
| | | At or below minimum wage | | |
		Total	At minimum wage	Below minimum wage
Under 25 years	16,275	814	145	669
16 to 19 years	5,434	373	93	280
20 to 24 years	10,841	441	52	389
25 years and over	59,597	915	122	793

Taken from: "Characteristics of Minimum Wage Workers: 2007," U.S. Bureau of Labor, May 7, 2008. www.bis.gov/cps/minwage2007tbls.htm#7.

race. He is also vice president of his student council, an attorney in the school's mock trial competitions and an elder at his church. In addition, he spent the past few months volunteering at night and on the weekends for Beau Biden, son of [U.S. Vice President] Joseph Biden, in Beau's successful bid to become attorney general of Delaware.

"My dream is to become the president of the United States," Tim says with pride, and he's doing everything he thinks will get him on the path to greatness—except holding down a paying job.

His mother, Sally McBride, likes it that way. She has encouraged her son to concentrate on academics and extracurricular activities that will help propel him in his career. A job, she says, is not a priority.

Work Not in the Cards

This holiday season, teens nationwide won't be fighting each other for mall jobs. Since the 1970s, the focus on education by parents and students has meant a declining number of teens following help-wanted signs. [In 2005], 43.7% of teens were employed or looking for work, the lowest since the U.S. government began collecting the data in 1948.

The decline is not only among teenagers whose families are in the middle- and upper-middle classes. Studies show that the number of teens from all socioeconomic levels in the workforce has been declining, says Daniel Aaronson, a senior economist at the Federal Reserve Bank of Chicago.

The trend means that teens such as Tim are missing out on a key experience. According to research I've conducted for my book, which includes interviews with more than 50 CEOs [chief executive officers] and leaders from all walks of life about the lessons they learned during childhood and early careers, punching a clock leaves a lasting, valuable mark.

Values of Working

Jeylan Mortimer, professor of sociology at the University of Minnesota, tracked 1,000 high school students and found that by their 20s, those who had held jobs in their teens developed better interpersonal skills and confidence than those who had bypassed teen toil.

Also, many of the nation's top CEOs worked in their teens. Matt Blank, of Showtime Networks Inc., told me that his first job at age 16 was working in a store's lingerie department making $3 an hour. He was fired for not following orders. "I was devastated," he recalls. His lesson: "The work world isn't always fair."

Tom Glocer, CEO of Reuters Group PLC, says his stint as a bike messenger at age 17 (in which he was treated like dirt) changed the way he looked at things. "They assumed I was a drop-out and stealing cars in my spare time." His lesson: "You never know who you're dealing with," so "treat people with respect regardless of their positions."

Another priceless lesson these leaders said they learned was that money doesn't grow on trees.

Tim's parents pay for his cellphone; they bought him an iPod for his birthday and give him spending money if he wants to go to the movies with friends.

Studies have shown that teens who work have better interpersonal skills and more confidence than their peers who do not work.

"I've spoiled him," Sally McBride admits. "If he could fit a job in, it would be a valuable lesson because I don't think he knows the value of a dollar."

As a mother of a 7-year-old and a 4-year-old, who are probably already a bit self indulgent, I'm hoping our children will be not only book-smart but also working stiffs during their teen years.

SIXTEEN

Teens Should Not Have Jobs

Amitai Etzioni

In the following selection Amitai Etzioni argues that working at part-time jobs, such as at McDonald's, is not a good thing for teens. These jobs are not educational and do not teach any kind of useful skills, notes Etzioni. He cites figures that show that teens work too many hours and too many days per week for there to be no effect on schoolwork. Etzioni also points out that teens learn bad habits when it comes to spending the money they make at their jobs. Etzioni is the director of the Institute for Communitarian Policy Studies at The George Washington University.

McDonald's is bad for your kids. I do not mean the flat patties and the white-flour buns; I refer to the jobs teen-agers undertake, mass-producing these choice items.

As many as two-thirds of America's high-school juniors and seniors now hold down part-time paying jobs, according to studies. Many of these are in fast-food chains, of which McDonald's is the pioneer, trend-setter and symbol.

At first, such jobs may seem right out of the Founding Fathers' educational manual for how to bring up self-reliant, work-ethic-driven, productive youngsters. But in fact, these jobs undermine school attendance and involvement, impart few skills that will be useful in later life, and simultaneously skew the values of teenagers—especially their ideas about the worth of a dollar.

It has been a long-standing American tradition that youngsters ought to get paying jobs. In folklore, few pursuits are more deeply revered than the newspaper route and the sidewalk lemonade stand. Here the youngsters are to learn how sweet are the fruits of labor and self-discipline (papers are delivered early in the morning, rain or shine) and the ways of trade (if you price your lemonade too high or too low. . .).

A Highly Uneducational Job

Roy Rogers, Baskin Robbins, Kentucky Fried Chicken, et al., may at first seem nothing but a vast extension of the lemonade stand. They provide very large numbers of teen jobs, provide regular employment, pay quite well compared to many other teen jobs and, in the modern equivalent of toiling over a hot stove, test one's stamina.

Closer examination, however, finds the McDonald's kind of job highly uneducational in several ways. Far from providing opportunities for entrepreneurship (the lemonade stand) or self-discipline, self-supervision and self-scheduling (the paper route), most teen jobs these days are highly structured—what social scientists call "highly routinized."

True, you still have to have the gumption to get yourself over to the hamburger stand, but once you don the prescribed uniform, your task is spelled out in minute detail. The franchise prescribes the shape of the coffee cups; the weight, size, shape and color of the patties; and the texture of the napkins (if any). Fresh coffee is to be made every eight minutes. And so on. There is no room for initiative, creativity or even elementary rearrangements. These are breeding grounds for robots working for yesterday's assembly lines, not tomorrow's high-tech posts.

There are very few studies of the matter. One is a 1984 study by Ivan Charner and Bryna Shore Fraser. It relies mainly on what teen-agers write in response to questionnaires rather than actual observations of fast-food jobs. The authors argue that the employees develop many skills, such as how to operate a food-preparation machine and a cash register. However, little attention is paid to how long it takes to acquire such a skill, or what its significance is. What does it matter if you spend 20 minutes learning to use a cash register and then "operate" it? What "skill" have you acquired? It is a long way from learning to work with a lathe or carpenter tools in the olden days or to program computers in the modern age.

A 1980 study by A.V. Harrell and P.W. Wirtz found that, among those students who worked at least 25 hours per week while in school, their unemployment rate four years later was half of that of seniors who did not work. This is an impressive statistic. It must be seen, though, together with the finding that many who begin as part-time employees in fast-food chains drop out of high school and are gobbled up in the world of low-skill jobs.

Some say that while these jobs are rather unsuited for college-bound, white, middle-class youngsters, they are "ideal" for lower-class, "non-academic", minority youngsters. Indeed, minorities are "over-represented" in these jobs (21 percent of fast-food employees). While it is true that these places provide income, work and even some training to such youngsters, they also tend to perpetuate their disadvantaged status. They provide no career ladders and few marketable skills, and they undermine school attendance and involvement.

The hours are often long. Among those 14 to 17, a third of fast-food employees (including some school drop-outs) labor more than 30 hours per week, according to the Charner-Fraser study. Only 20 percent work 15 hours or less. The rest: between 15 and 30 hours. Often the restaurants close late, and after closing one must clean up and tally up. In affluent Montgomery County [Maryland], where child labor would not seem to be a widespread economic necessity, 24 percent of the seniors at Walt Whitman High School in 1985 worked as much as five to seven days a week; 27 percent, three to five. There is just no way such amounts of work will not interfere with school work, especially homework. In an informal survey published in the most recent Walt Whitman

For teens who work long hours in fast-food chains, their schoolwork suffers, and, for many of them, dropping out of school may be the result.

yearbook, 58 percent of the seniors acknowledged that their jobs interfere with their school work.

The Charner-Fraser study sees merit in learning teamwork and working under supervision. The authors have a point here. However, it must be noted that such learning is not automatically educational or wholesome. For example, much of the supervision in fast-food places leans toward teaching one the wrong kinds of compliance: blind obedience, or shared alienation with the "boss."

Supervision is often both tight and woefully inappropriate. Today, fast-food chains and other such places of work (record shops, bowling alleys) keep costs down by having teens supervise teens, often with no adult on the premises. There is no father or mother figure with which to identify, to emulate, to provide a role model and guidance. The work-culture varies from one place to another: Sometimes it is a tightly run shop (must keep the cash registers ringing); sometimes a rather loose pot party interrupted by customers. However, only rarely is there a master to learn from, or much worth learning. Indeed, far from being places where solid adult work values are being transmitted, these are places where all too often delinquent teen values dominate. Typically, when my son Oren was dishing out ice cream for Baskin Robbins in upper Manhattan, his fellow teen-workers considered him a sucker for not helping himself to the till. Most youngsters felt they were entitled to $50 severance "pay" on their last day on the job.

Where Does the Money Go?

The pay, oddly, is the part of the teen work-world which is most difficult to evaluate. The lemonade stand or paper route money was for your allowance. In the old days, apprentices learning a trade from a master contributed most, if not all, of their income to their parents' household. Today, the teen pay may be low by adult standards, but it is often, especially in the middle class, spent largely or wholly by the teens. That is, the youngsters live free at home, ("after all, they are high school kids") and are left with very substantial sums of money.

Where this money goes is not quite clear. Some use it to support themselves, especially among the poor. More middle class kids set some money aside to help pay for college, or save it for a major purchase—often a car. But large amounts seem to flow to pay for an early introduction into the most trite aspects of American consumerism: Flimsy punk clothes, trinkets and whatever else is the last fast-moving teen craze.

One may say that this is only fair and square; they are being good American consumers, working and spending their money on what turns them on. At least, a cynic might add, these funds do not go into illicit drugs and booze. On the other hand, an educator might bemoan that these young, yet unformed individuals, so early in life are driven to buy objects of no intrinsic educational, cultural or social merit, learn so quickly the dubious merit of keeping up with the Joneses in ever-changing fads promoted by mass merchandising.

Many teens find the instant reward of money, and the youth status symbols it buys, much more alluring than credits in calculus courses, European history, or foreign languages. No wonder quite a few would rather skip school—and certainly homework—and instead work longer at a Burger King. Thus, most teen work these days is not providing early lessons in work ethic; it fosters escape from school and responsibilities, quick gratification and a short cut to the consumeristic aspects of adult life.

Part of the List of Social Problems

Thus, ironically, we must add youth employment, not merely unemployment, to our list of social problems. And, like many other social ills, the unfortunate aspects of teen work resist easy correction. Sure, it would be much better if corporations that

The Five Most Dangerous Teen Jobs

1.	Agriculture: fieldwork and processing
2.	Traveling youth crews
3.	Construction and work at heights
4.	Driver/operator: forklifts, tractors, and ATVs
5.	Outside helper: landscaping, groundskeeping, and lawn service

Many teens work at exhausting, low-paying positions in places such as fast-food restaurants. However, they may also find themselves working in more perilous jobs.

Taken from: "NCL's 2008 Five Worst Teen Jobs," National Consumers League. www.nclnet.org/labor/childlabor/jobreport2008.htm.

employ teens would do so in conjunction with high schools and school districts. Educators could help define what is the proper amount of gainful work (not more than "X" hours per school week); how late kids may be employed on school nights (not later than 9 p.m.), encourage employer understanding during exam periods, and insist on proper supervision. However, corporations are extremely unlikely to accept such an approach which, in effect, would curb their ability to draw on a major source of cheap labor. And, in these laissez faire days, Congress is quite disinclined to pass new social legislation forcing corporations to be more attentive to the education needs of the minors they so readily employ.

Schools might extend their own work-study programs (starting their own franchises?!) but, without corporate help, these are unlikely to amount to much. Luckily, few schools (less than 10 percent) provide any credit for such work experience. But schools that do should insist that they will provide credit for work only if it meets their educational standards; only if they are consulted on matters such as supervision and on-the-job training; and only if their representatives are allowed to inspect the places of employment. School counselors should guide the youngsters only to those places of work that are willing to pay attention to educational elements of these jobs.

Parents who are still willing to take their role seriously may encourage their youngsters to seek jobs at places that are proper work settings and insist that fast-food chains and other franchises shape up or not employ their kids. Also an agreement should be reached with the youngsters that a significant share of teen earnings should be dedicated to the family, or saved for agreed-upon items.

Above all, parents should look at teen employment not as automatically educational. It is an activity—like sports—that can be turned into an educational opportunity. But it can also easily be abused. Youngsters must learn to balance the quest for income with the needs to keep growing and pursue other endeavors which do not pay off instantly—above all education.

Go back to school.

What You Should Know About Money Management

Students and Credit Cards

- More high schoolers use debit cards than credit cards. In a 2008 survey, 53.3 percent of high schoolers polled had a debit card, up from 35.9 percent in 2002. Only 34.7 percent used a credit card, up from 32.2 percent in 2002.
- 82 percent of college students carry a monthly credit card debt of under $1000.
- 10 percent of college students carry a balance of over $7,800.
- The average college student's credit card debt is $3,200.
- One-third of college students say that they accumulated more than $10,000 of credit card debt while in school.
- 68 percent of teens say they have never discussed responsible credit card use with their parents.
- Teens who use prepaid cards most frequently use them at fast-food restaurants, followed by grocery stores, gas stations, restaurants, and movie theaters.
- Teens who use prepaid cards spend the most money at clothing stores, followed by other specialty retail stores, bookstores, and discount stores.

Teens' Saving and Spending

- Teens in America spend $158 billion a year.
- More than $2 billion a year is spent advertising to teens.

- Males spend more on video games; females spend more on clothes.
- 17 percent of teens say they spend most of their money as soon as they get it, 24 percent save all of their money, and 59 percent usually save half of their money.
- 26 percent of teens say that they frequently discuss saving for a college education with their families.
- 57 percent of teens say that a parent or relative opened a savings account for them.
- 41 percent of teens ask a relative or parent for investing or saving advice.
- 30 percent of teens who are saving money are saving for a car.
- 13 percent of teens think the best way to save is to put their money in a piggy bank.
- 12 percent of teens own stock, and 12 percent own mutual funds.
- 49 percent of teens said they would like to learn more about money management.
- 76 percent of parents say that money management skills should be taught in schools.

Teens and Jobs

- 72 percent of teens report doing odd jobs to earn money.
- 34 percent of older teens have a full- or part-time job.
- Teens make up 3.82 percent of the workforce.
- Teens aged sixteen to nineteen make up 21.6 percent of the people earning minimum wage.
- As of July 2009, federal minimum wage is $7.25 an hour.
- Teens get injured on the job two to three times more often than adults.
- Teens who work in restaurants are the most likely teen workers to be injured on the job.
- Less than 25 percent of teens earn enough to get what they want without financial help from their parents.
- In 2008, the teen joblessness rate was higher than it had been in sixty years.

What You Should Do About Money Management

Money management skills are always important but, with the fluxes in the economy in recent years, having solid money management skills is crucial. The first step to mastering money management is to get a handle on your own finances. The best way to do this is to start a budget. A budget does not have to be complicated. Simply write down all your sources of income (allowance, job, gifts, etc.) and keep track of all your expenses for a month. Write down everything you purchase, and you will get a clear picture of where your money is going. It can be surprising to realize what you are really spending your money on. A daily soda at a fast-food restaurant, for example, can add up to quite a lot over a period of a month. When you have your data, label your expenses as either fixed or variable. Fixed expenses are ones you have to pay, such as school costs. Variable expenses are ones that you can control, like eating out or going to the movies.

Making Changes

If you do not like how the numbers add up at the end of the month, you have a few options. You can figure out how to make more money, you can cut your variable expenses, or you can do both. There will probably be a few expenses you can cut right away. Cutting other expenses may be more tricky and require some hard decisions. Would it be worth it to cut down on certain small items if you knew you were saving for something bigger? Money is a tool for your life—figure out how you want it to work for you. Do you want to save for a car? For college? A computer? When you have a goal clearly in mind, it is easier to forgo smaller luxuries because you know what you are saving for.

Make sure that you budget a little extra "fun" money for yourself that you can use however you want. It is easier to stick with a budget if you give yourself a little leeway. Budgeting is not about deprivation, it is about getting control over your money.

Negotiating a Higher Allowance

If, after changing your spending habits, you find that you still want more money coming in, you might approach your family about an allowance increase. Parents tend to respond best to an organized, reasoned approach. You will have a better chance if you show them your budget and document why a bigger allowance is a good idea. If they are not receptive to raising your allowance, they might be more willing to an increase if you agree to take on more chores. Negotiate something that works for everyone. If you already get a weekly allowance, you might suggest a monthly one instead. With a monthly allowance, you will have more opportunity to hone your budgeting skills and plan ahead for purchases. Remember, though, that a monthly allowance requires more self-discipline. If you are the kind of person who tends to spend the whole amount immediately and then suffer for the rest of the month, this is not the plan for you.

Get a Job

You might not be old enough for some jobs, but there are still a lot of ways teens can make money. Teen jobs such as dog sitting, babysitting, house-sitting, yard work and doing chores for neighbors are old favorites and are worth looking into. They do not require much more start-up cost than printing up a few flyers and handing them to people you know. If these jobs do not appeal to you, find something more tailored to your special skills. You can create your own job based on your expertise. Are you a talented writer? Offer your services as a family biographer. Are you gifted with a camera? Offer to be the official photographer or videographer for someone's big event, like a birthday or anniversary. Let your talents work for you. Sports-minded teens can offer one-on-one coaching, scholastically inclined teens can tutor younger students, and musicians can give music lessons. Be creative in brainstorming ideas to make money.

Educate Yourself

If you understand the basics of budgeting and have a good handle on your own finances, you have made a great start. But there is a lot more to money management than just that. To get to the next level, you will need to learn about savings and investing. There are plenty of ways to get smart about money. Check out Web sites that are designed for teens, such as TeenAnalyst (www.teenanalyst.com). The Motley Fool (www.motleyfool.com) also has a lot of articles and advice geared toward teens. Find books in the library on saving and investing. You can also learn a lot from watching one of the money networks on TV such as CNBC and by reading the business section of the newspaper. There might be adults in your life who can talk to you about investing and making financial decisions. There are also classes and financial camps, where teens can go to learn about saving and investing. A Web search using the term "financial camps" will yield a large list.

ORGANIZATIONS TO CONTACT

The editors have compiled the following list of organizations concerned with the issues debated in this book. The descriptions are derived from materials provided by the organizations. All have publications or information available for interested readers. The list was compiled on the date of publication of the present volume; the information provided here may change. Be aware that many organizations take several weeks or longer to respond to inquiries, so allow as much time as possible.

BetterInvesting
PO Box 220, Royal Oak, MI 48068
(248) 583-6242 • toll-free: (877) 275-6242 • fax: (248) 583-4880
e-mail: service@betterinvesting.org
Web site: www.betterinvesting.org

BetterInvesting, the nation's largest nonprofit organization dedicated to investment education, is run by the National Association of Investors Corporation (NAIC). BetterInvesting provides investing knowledge and practical investing experience through local investment clubs, local chapters, online courses, and an active online community. It also offers advice geared specifically toward teens. The group publishes *BetterInvesting Magazine*.

Consumer Jungle
103 Palouse St., Ste. 35, Wenatchee, WA 98807
(509) 663-3685 • toll-free (866) 282-4652
Web site: www.consumerjungle.org

Consumer Jungle is an interactive, Web-based program that helps high school students become smart consumers. Its Web site provides consumer education curricula covering a variety of topics, including credit cards, cell phones, personal finances, and consumer fraud. The site also has a section for students featuring quizzes, games, and worksheets. Consumer Jungle publishes the *Junglevine Newsletter*.

The Jump$tart Coalition for Personal Financial Literacy
919 Eighteenth St. NW, Ste. 300 Washington, DC 20006
(888) 45-EDUCATE • fax: (202) 223-0321
e-mail: info@jumpstartcoalition.org
Web site: www.jumpstartcoalition.org/

Jump$tart is a national coalition of organizations dedicated to improving the financial literacy of kindergarten through college-age youth by providing advocacy, research, standards, and educational resources. Jump$tart's Web site offers tools such as "The Reality Check" test designed to teach students what they will need to do to reach their financial goals. Jump$tart publishes the quarterly newsletter *Jump$tart Update*.

Junior Achievement (JA)
One Education Way, Colorado Springs, CO 80906
(719) 540-8000 • fax: (719) 540-6299
e-mail: newmedia@ja.org
Web site: www.ja.org

Junior Achievement is dedicated to educating students about workforce readiness, entrepreneurship, and financial literacy through experiential, hands-on programs. The organization uses community volunteers who use their own experiences to teach students about business and financial issues. JA publishes a quarterly magazine, *Futures*.

National Consumers League (NCL)
1701 K St. NW, Ste. 1200, Washington, DC 20006
(202) 835-3323 • fax: (202) 835-0747
e-mail info@nclnet.org
Web site: www.nclnet.org

NCL is the oldest U.S. consumer organization. The group works to protect consumers' rights and promote justice in the workplace.

It runs several offshoot Web sites, including www.fraud.org and stopchildlabor.org. NCL publishes a variety of brochures, fact sheets, and newsletters, including the brochure for teen workers "Is This the Job for You?"

National Endowment for Financial Education (NEFE)
5299 DTC Blvd., Ste. 1300, Greenwood Village, CO 80111
(303) 741-6333 • fax: (303) 220-0838
Web site: www.nefe.org

NEFE is a national nonprofit organization dedicated to improving the financial well-being of Americans. The organization offers a variety of services, including materials for educators, research for consumers and think tanks, and free financial assistance to those who cannot afford a financial adviser. NEFE's High School Financial Planning Program includes a Web site, http://hsfpp. nefe.org/home, which has games, calculators, and articles for teens interested in financial issues. NEFE publishes the newsletter *NEFE Digest*.

YoungBiz
5053 Ocean Blvd., Ste. 104, Siesta Key, FL 34242
toll-free: (888) 543-7929
e-mail: steve_morris@mindspring.com
Web site: www.youngbiz.com

The mission of YoungBiz is "to empower youth with entrepreneurial, business, and financial skills through innovative education and real-world experience." YoungBiz offers camps and workshops for teens, teacher training, and curricula on issues of money and business. The group's Web site publishes articles on business, entrepreneurship, and personal finance.

Young Money
10950 Gilroy Rd., Ste. D, Hunt Valley, MD 21031
toll-free (888) 788-4335 x1 • fax: (443) 264-0277

e-mail: cara@youngmoney.com
Web site: www.youngmoney.com

Young Money is a national organization specializing in personal finance education for young people. The group's Web site offers information on various aspects of money management, including financial aid, credit, debt, and careers. Young Money publishes a magazine written primarily by student journalists, *Young Money*.

BIBLIOGRAPHY

Books

Katherine R. Bateman, *The Young Investor: Projects and Activities for Making Your Money Grow*. Chicago: Chicago Review, 2001.

Jessica Blatt, with Variny Paladino, *The Teen Girl's Gotta-Have-It Guide to Money: Getting Smart About Making It, Saving It, and Spending It!* New York: Watson-Guptill, 2007.

Sanyika Calloway Boyce, *Teen Money Tips: Simple Steps for Banking, Saving and Making Money*. New York: Smart Concepts, 2003.

Kathryn R. Deering, *Cash and Credit Information for Teens: Tips for a Successful Financial Life*. Detroit: Omnigraphics, 2005.

Debby Fowles, *1000 Best Smart Money Secrets for Students*. Naperville, IL: Sourcebooks, 2005.

David and Tom Gardner, with Selena Maranjian, *The Motley Fool Investment Guide for Teens: 8 Steps to Having More Money than Your Parents Ever Dreamed Of*. Topeka, KS: Topeka Bindery, 2003.

Robert T. Kiyosaki, with Sharon L. Lechter, *Rich Dad Poor Dad for Teens: The Secrets About Money—That You Don't Learn in School!* New York: Little, Brown Young Readers, 2004.

Susan Knox, *Financial Basics: Money-Management Guide for Students*. Columbus: Ohio State University Press, 2004.

Susan Shelley, *Complete Idiot's Guide to Money for Teens*. New York: Alpha, 2001.

Farnoosh Torabi, *You're So Money: Live Rich, Even When You're Not*. New York: Three Rivers, 2008.

Periodicals

Janet Bodnar, "Expand 'Tween Allowances and Set Guidelines on Spending," Washingtonpost.com, September 14, 2008. www.washingtonpost.com/wp-dyn/content/article/2008/09/13/AR2008091300354.html?sid=ST2008092302068&s_pos=list.

Lisa Brown, "Teen with a Credit Card Doesn't Have to Be Scary," *Charleston (SC) Post and Courier*, February 19, 2008. www.charleston.net/news/2008/feb/19/teen_credit_card_doesnt_have_be_scary31057/.

Jonathan Burton, "What Teens Need to Know About Money," MarketWatch, May 14, 2007. www.marketwatch.com/News/Story/Story.aspx?guid=%7B181A02BD-699E-4DFD-A231-DD5BEF871E26%7D&siteid=nbk.

Anne D'Innocenzio, "Teens Turn to Thrift as Jobs Vanish and Prices Rise," *USA Today*, April 25, 2008. www.usatoday.com/money/economy/2008-04-19-teen-recession_N.htm.

Christine Evans, "As Parents Toil to Make Ends Meet, Teens' Carefree Days Meet an End," *Palm Beach (FL) Post*, August 23, 2008. www.palmbeachpost.com/news/content/local_news/epaper/2008/08/23/a1a_kids_squeeze_0824.html.

Sadie Gurman, "Whom Should Students Trust for Money Advice?" Young Money, February 27, 2006. www.youngmoney.com/money_management/budgeting/060227.

Barbara Hagenbaugh, "Full Activity, Study Schedules Have Many Teens Just Saying No to Jobs," *USA Today*, April 6, 2005. www.usatoday.com/money/economy/employment/2005-04-06-teen-work-usat_x.htm.

Froma Harrop, "Jobs for Teens: A Stimulating Idea," *Seattle Times*, June 2, 2008. http://seattletimes.nwsource.com/html/editorialsopinion/2004448808_harrop31.html.

Harriet Johnson-Brackey, "A Little Money, Lots of Time Can Make Teen a Millionaire," South Florida Sun-Sentinel.com, June 3, 2007. www.sun-sentinel.com/business/sns-yourmoney-0603teens,0,2104318.story.

Steve Last, "The Case for Prepaid Credit Cards for Teenagers," Buzzle.com, May 15, 2008. www.buzzle.com/articles/the-case-for-prepaid-credit-cards-for-teenagers.html.

Laval University Consumer Studies students and University of Ottawa Civil Law students, "The Financial Guide for Teenagers:

Thirteen- to Fifteen-Year-Olds," Office of the Superintendent of Bankruptcy Canada, December 5, 2008. www.ic.gc.ca/epic/site/bsf-osb.nsf/en/br01652e.html.

Kaitlin Manry, "Economy Forces Teens to Cope with Smaller Allowances, Lost Jobs," HeraldNet, November 17, 2008. www.heraldnet.com/article/20081117/NEWS01/711179873.

Angela Moore, "Are the Kids All Right? Teen Spending Slowdown Is a Bad Sign," MarketWatch, April 10, 2008. www.marketwatch.com/news/story/kids-all-right-teen-spending/story.aspx?guid=%7BA951C27A-834E-440E-B162-0EA461610FF6%7D.

Joe Morgan, "Credit Card Firm Targets Teens," TimesOnline, January 26, 2006. www.timesonline.co.uk/tol/money/borrowing/article720146.ece.

Mary Pilon, "Hello Muddah, Hello Fadduh, My Portfolio Is in the Gutter," *Wall Street Journal*, July 2, 2008. http://online.wsj.com/article/SB121495019809220955.html.

Scott Reeves, "Why Money Mistakes Matter," Minyanville, July 1, 2008. www.minyanville.com/articles/index.php?a=17806.

Laura Robertson, "Learn How to Manage Your Money Now, and You'll Be on Stronger Financial Footing When You're an Adult," *Knoxville (TN) News Sentinel*, August 26, 2008. www.knoxnews.com/news/2008/Aug/26/wealth-of-knowledge/.

J.M. Seymour, "Even Smart Students Are Financially Illiterate," SchoolFinder, September 13, 2008. http://schoolfinder.globalscholar.com/blog/493/even-smart-students-are-financially-illiterate/.

James Stephenson, "9 Ideas for Teen Businesses," Entrepreneur.com, April 11, 2006. www.entrepreneur.com/startingabusiness/teenstartups/article159548.html.